THE HEART OF THE CIRCLE

THE HEART OF THE CIRCLE
A GUIDE TO DRUMMING

By
Holly Blue Hawkins

Foreword by
Brooke Medicine Eagle

THE CROSSING PRESS
FREEDOM, CALIFORNIA

Copyright © 1999 by Holly Blue Hawkins
Cover design by Tara M. Phillips
Cover photographs by Patricia Hinz
Excerpt from Lou Harrison's percussion trio, *Tributes to Charon*. (From Leta Miller, ed. *Lou Harrison: Selected Keyboard and Chamber Music, 1937-1994*, in *Music in the United States of America 8* [Madison, WI: A-R Editions, 1998]. Used by permission.)
Printed in the U.S.A.

For information on bulk purchases or group discounts for this and other Crossing Press titles, please contact our Special Sales Manager at 800/777-1048.**www.crossingpress.com**

If you would like to contact Holly Blue Hawkins you can write her at P.O. Box 2094, Aptos, CA 95001 or email her at hollyblue@earthlink.net.

Library of Congress Cataloging-in-Publication Data

Hawkins, Holly Blue.
　　The heart of the circle : a guide to drumming / by Holly Blue Hawkins.
　　　　p. cm.
　　Includes bibliographical references.
　　ISBN 1-58091-025-4 (pbk.)
　　1. Drum--Instruction and study. 2. Drum--Religious aspects. 3. Spiritual life--New Age Movement. I. Title.
　　MT662.H39　　1999
　　786.9'192--dc21　　　　　　　　　　　　　　　　99-33918
　　　　　　　　　　　　　　　　　　　　　　　　　　　　CIP

ACKNOWLEDGMENTS

The stories, people, and lessons in this book are the very fabric of my life. I want to say thank you to *everyone* who has influenced my journey and participated in the events retold in these pages, especially all the novice drummers who asked for more.

Special thanks first of all, to my parents for supporting my work, nurturing my spirit, and raising me in an environment rich with words, music, imagination, and reverence for all life.

To Brooke Medicine Eagle, who shines a navigational beacon and the bright light of inspiration, thank you for a deep and thoughtful reading of the first draft—you will see I have taken your good counsel, again.

To Heidrun Hoffmann—visionary, master drummer, teacher, and friend—and to all the DiRRiD folk, especially Margaret More, Peter Greenwood, Debra Houston, Pilar Marti, and Joyce Lounsberry.

To Patty Hinz for photographs, feedback, and friendship. To Kai deFontenay for providing The Mountain, the trailer, and a home.

To Leta Miller for reading parts of the manuscript and providing greater musical depth—not to mention a stack of articles—inspiration, and the rich experience of singing in the Temple Beth El Choir. To Jamie Rackley for reading and wrestling with the entire manuscript, for your depth, insights, honesty, and humor. To Cantor Paula Marcus and Rabbi Richard Litvak for help with the chapter on ceremony—among other things! To Grandma Bertha Grove, for generously sharing wisdom, experience, and a loving heart.

For granting the privilege to quote, thanks to:
Rachel Naomi Remen and Riverhead Books
Christina Baldwin and Bantam Books
Lou Harrison and the American Musicological Society

To Elaine Goldman Gill, Caryle Hirshberg, and Eleanor Piazza of The Crossing Press for believing in this project. To Jeanne Rosen and Richard Klein for valuable time, insight, support, expertise, and guidance into the world of writers. And to Rita Mae Brown, for writing *Starting From Scratch*.

To all the Santa Cruz County drum buddies, especially Raya Bullard, Janice Skinner, Ken Kimes, and Sandra Green. To Romilly Grauer and Janine Talty for giving me back my body after a devastating injury—making it possible for me to write and drum again. To Lee Schiff for providing an exquisite place to live and work. To Rodney Scott for his vision and impeccability in bringing Mother Drums into the world, especially our *Heart of Peace*, and to everyone who contributed time, energy, and support toward bringing this drum into the world. To Wendy B. Walsh for opening doors. To Janet Guttridge for going *beyond*. And to Susan Brown, for handing me my first guitar.

To Karin Adam, Nena Van Velzor, Jonah Van Adam, Carol Drexler, Jim Cormier, and Delorme McKee-Stovall, for all your support, enthusiasm, curiosity, and love. To Jennyfurface and Katmandu, for enduring the boring life of a writer's familiar.

Finally, to my partner Jo Koven, who has been here through it all: for being my favorite drumming partner, helping to bend wet wood into rims, schlepping drums to beaches and hilltops, questioning me into deeper understanding, catching the first seed ideas of this book in shorthand on Highway 101 somewhere south of Wild Horse, stopping for owls, making sure there was always tahini, reminding me to walk or skate or eat, leaving me to my process.

And to the Great Imagination for imagining this.

For Jonah

In Memory of
Susan Seddon Boulet

CONTENTS

And Miriam the prophetess, the sister of Aaron,
took a timbrel in her hand;
and all the women went out after her
with timbrels and with dances.

FoReWoRD

When I think of Holly, I see her sitting at the Mother Drum in the center of my teaching circles, drumming the heartbeat for the entire time I am working with the group. This seems so simple—like it has always been this way—yet it has taken many years to come to this very special place.

I first met Holly when she sponsored my work in Hawaii many years ago; we made an instant and deep connection of spirit. Later, when she moved to the mainland, she helped me with my first Eagle Song Camp, and assisted at the Drum Gatherings I was doing then. The song of my big Mother Drum called to her heart, and she became fascinated with drumming. Eventually she was able to help make one of these drums for herself and began helping my brother Rodney create these wonderful drums for people all around the country.

With her Mother Drum, *Heart of Peace*, she began calling drum circles together. Later Holly began to study rhythm and dance with Heidrun Hoffmann and, through her practice and intent, developed into a fine drummer. I've watched her gather inexperienced workshop participants and make them into a solid and powerful drum group in a very short while. And, most special of all, I have observed her inviting a bashful person into the circle and taking extra time to introduce him to the drum in such a way that he learned to love drumming and feel at home with it. Thus, Holly has become a fine and gifted teacher.

From this place of heartfelt excitement and experience, as well as willingness to share, Holly comes to you through this book. The techniques she offers are vitally important now when we as two-leggeds are so scattered and uncentered.

Community drums have called people all over the world to come together since time immemorial. They have set the rhythm for a dance of life, which is harmonious and unified. They have reminded people of the heartbeat of Mother Earth, which lives in us all and reminds us of our oneness with all of life. As we are awakening again to the power and necessity of this unity with All Our Relations, the drum is coming to the forefront of our consciousness. Yet, most of us are beginners in making, holding, and caring for these special beings. Into this gap Holly steps with clear and specific ways to help us move forward into this communion at all its levels.

I have a vision that some day every community will be built again around a center where people gather in unity, friendship, council, dancing, and celebration. There is always a Mother Drum there, calling the people and setting the rhythm of their coming together. The drum's heartbeat is vital to the health and well-being of the people; in this book, Holly is the drum's spokesperson. Listen well and come into the dance of wholeness and holiness with All Our Relations. The children of all beings for seven generations following us will benefit.

—Brooke Medicine Eagle

INTRODUCTION

Rhythm is all around us: windshield wipers dancing in a storm, the urgency of electrical impulses through wires, the steady pulsation of the planet. Some rhythms have a centering, healing effect on us while others, particularly the high-frequency vibrations so much a part of our modern world, can cause anxiety and dis-ease. Before we are born, before we are even conceived, we dwell in a world of pulsations. We incubate mere inches from the thunderous presence of our mother's heartbeat, massaged by the surging tide of her blood, the expansion and contraction of her bodily functions, the rocking motion of her stride.

Close your eyes and listen. What do you hear? Perhaps it's a snappy tune you heard on the radio, the sound of your heart beating, or your feet crunching through snow—even the leaky faucet you only remember in the wee hours of the morning. Life is full of rhythm. The more you tune into it, the more it will come and find you

There was a time when music belonged to everyone. Somehow the Industrial Age has forced us into such exaggerated specialization we now tend to think that, unless we are expert in something, we shouldn't do it at all. Our soul cries out for music, so we pop in a CD and listen to a recording of someone else making music for us.

But what would it be like if, instead, *you* picked up a drum, or a rattle, or some other musical instrument and started to express *yourself*? At first it might be very frustrating, so much so, that you want to give up and go back to that vicarious

CD experience. But what if you stuck with it, evicted your inner critic from the audience in your head, and just explored whatever wanted to come out? Imagine yours are the hands on a musical instrument being played by some invisible *other.* What would it sound like, and more importantly what would it *feel* like? And how would *you* feel afterwards?

What if you knew nothing of drums and drumming? What if, like the apes in *2001: A Space Odyssey*, you were one day surprised by this mysterious object, and began to explore it with curiosity. How does it feel in your hands? How do you hold it? What can it do? How many different kinds of sound can it make? Tap, stroke, and caress it. Tickle it with your fingernails. Thump its sides with the heel of your hand. What makes it sing, hum, giggle? Braille your way around the surface like a map, and test the different regions. Do they all sound the same, or can you make different sounds at the edge than in the center? Start a dialogue between those sounds—a call and response—swinging like the pendulum of a grandfather clock, back and forth, back and forth, "du-dung, bip-bip, du-dung, bip-bip."

Try this if you like: stand up, and rock from one foot to the other, as if you were going for a stroll, *yum-bah-yum-bah*. Now see if you can hum along, perhaps imitating the rhythm of your feet, or weaving playfully in between the steady *yum-bah-yum-bah*. Then put an emphasis on one side: *YUM-bah-YUM-bah*. Or, *yum-BAH-yum-BAH*. Two left feet? No problem! Just name one of them "Yum" and the other "Bah" and keep going. Rhythm can break if you drop it, but it can also bounce. Unlike a fragile dish, the minute you pick a rhythm up again, it's back. So you can think of rhythm as a sturdy container; it can hold whatever you put into it: a nursery rhyme or a symphony.

When I look back over my love affair with the drum, vivid images stand out in my mind. I return to the Black Tail Ranch, a jewel of a valley set in the green mountains of Montana. The first insinuation of dawn glowed behind the silhouette of mountains encircling the valley as I stepped from the council tipi. For several hours I had been drumming a steady heartbeat while most of the camp slept. A group of us had gathered at the Black Tail for a ceremony, and our whole community had agreed to drum 'round the clock for days by working in shifts.

Three of us played the great Mother Drum from 2:00 until 4:00 A.M., then continued on because somebody's alarm clock didn't sound. Sustaining the deceptively simple rhythm proved a challenging task, as we sat there in the firelight, trying neither to speed up nor slow down, but provide the steady "Mother-Mother-Mother" for the dream time of our companions who were sleeping in tents and RVs scattered across the valley. The need to control things, to do it right, tugged us this way and that. Several times one of the drummers silently stormed out of the tipi in frustration, only to return later calmed down and ready to try again.

I found it difficult to stop at dawn, though I was tired of sitting and ready for a nap. We three had grown so close during those nearly wordless hours spent together. As I stood before the tipi and greeted the new day, a single thought filled my mind: If world leaders had to drum together all night for their people before making important decisions, how different our world would be.

Why is it these things seem to happen at night?

I sat at my friend's bedside in a hospital ICU, watching the steady rise and fall of her chest as a respirator maintained the rhythmic flow of artificial breath. Although her brain had ceased to function, her heart kept beating steadily for days and days. The ordinary pace of my life had gone into suspended animation as I camped out in the hospital trying to make sense of what was happening to my friend. Half asleep, half in a trance from the respirator's hypnotic pace, I gazed at the machines and tubes and oscilloscope screen. Suddenly, I threw off my blanket, leapt from my chair and ran to the nurse's station. "I don't understand. Her heart keeps beating even though her brain isn't working. How can this be? I thought the brain ran the body."

What I learned that night changed my life. The brain does not run the heart. The nurse told me that the heart in essence has a "mind" of its own, and heart cells will continue beating outside the body. In fact, cells from two hearts in close proximity on a microscope slide will soon beat together.[1] So the romantic notion of "two hearts beating as one" isn't just a lover's fantasy. It really happens. When we drum, we can express and influence our own natural rhythms. Drumming together is a powerful means of unification—reaching beyond language and belief system—to bring people together through heart connection. When we drum together, our hearts begin to synchronize, to "beat as one."

This book was written for anyone who is interested in drumming. It provides the basic skills to allow even novice drummers to experience the joy of drumming alone or in a group. If you are a beginner, I hope you will feel supported and encouraged to experiment; but even trained percussionists may be surprised to discover untapped spiritual dimensions to deceptively simple rhythms.

The popularity of drumming in all forms and drum circles in particular is increasing. Most bookstores and catalogues that deal with personal growth and human potential include at least one drum in their product line. Many communities and college campuses have drum gatherings, some informal and spontaneous, as well as regular classes and events. This is no accident. We are instinctively drawn back to the fundamental element of life—and drumming is a means of communicating beyond words, in rhythm: the language of the heart.

Throughout this book you will find the word "circle" used to describe a particular kind of group. A group may happen by chance; a circle happens by intent. The circle is a structure, which is rich in symbolism. It is not a pyramid, or a box, or even a spiral. You can think of it in the sense of electricity. Each participant acts like a link in the circuit, as generator, transmitter, or resistor. Participants influence the "energy" of the circle by their attitude and focus. A circle also expresses the image of a container. We think in terms of inside and outside the circle. What is within the circle is held by each member, and by the whole. In shamanism there is a saying:

The moon is a circle, the sun is a circle, the Earth is a circle, the drum is a circle, and we are a circle.

A circle is a special kind of group, not because of what is done, but how it is done.

The Heart of the Circle responds to the needs of individuals and circles who are interested in integrating drumming into an existing spiritual practice, or want to use drumming as a vehicle for spiritual development. The approach is intentionally open-ended, reaching beyond the limits of any particular tradition, by defining the elements of ceremony from a cross-cultural perspective. We will explore different approaches to rhythm and kinds of drumming, and walk through the process of finding a drum, taking care of it, calling a circle, setting an intention, and drumming together. In the back of this book you will find a *Glossary* of terms you may find unfamiliar, and a *Resources* section to help you locate drums and other percussion instruments, teachers, and related subject matter.

Many times in conference and workshop settings I have had the following conversation:

"I wish I had a drum circle back home."

"Well, why don't you start one?"

"Oh, I don't know the first thing about drumming. I don't even own a drum."

"That's perfect! Then you won't get caught up in performance."

"But how will I know what to do?"

"Let the drum teach you."

Whether the skin of a drum is familiar territory to your hands or you have never so much as thumped a rhythm on a tabletop, this book is for you. It is an invitation to explore rhythm in a free and spontaneous manner and discover—or *re*discover—not only drumming, but also your own inner rhythms.

CHAPTER 1

GETTING STARTED

THE SEARCH FOR RHYTHM

Letting It In

When I start something new, the first hurdle is usually getting past the feeling that I don't know what I'm doing. I make things too hard. But do you suppose that when we were babies we spent much time contemplating the wobbliness of our knees before we ventured across the floor for the first time? There is simply something in us that *wants to walk*. If you picked up this book, chances are there is something in you that *wants to drum.*

When I was fifteen years old, I wanted to play the guitar more than anything else in the world. A neighbor was moving away and getting rid of everything she didn't consider worth the effort to pack. This included a funky old guitar with rusty strings and gummy varnish. It had been played so much there were dips in the fret board where sharp, steel strings had been dug into the wood by a strong hand. My friend carefully guided my fingertips into place and I walked home clutching the guitar's neck in a C chord for all I was worth, afraid that if I let go I would lose the precious cargo, my musical password.

I played that one chord over and over, strumming, plucking, testing all the possibilities, until it finally felt like a place I could find my way back to, my musical home base. Then I began to venture forth, lifting fingers one at a time, moving up and down the neck. By the time I went to bed that night, I could sing "Today While the Blossoms," accompanying myself with a few simple chords. My fingertips screamed from squeezing the strings into chords, but soon they became callused and tough. I learned many songs over the years, mostly by hanging out with other musicians, or sitting up front at concerts and focusing my attention on the guitarist's hands. I only took lessons for a short time, many years later, and don't remember much of what I learned.

The message? You don't have to be a trained expert to reap the benefits of expressing yourself through music, especially drumming. Although I am definitely a drummer, I wouldn't call myself a percussionist. I drummed, even led large drum circles, for years before I ever took up any formal study of drumming. Keep your eyes on the prize. Allow yourself to wander into that delicious space called beginner's mind[1] where there are no mistakes or missed notes, no inner critic, no performance, just freshness and an adventurous spirit. Enjoy the newness. Let it in.

Letting It Out

Our bodies are filled with pulsation and biorhythms. According to traditional Chinese medicine, there are twenty-seven recognizable pulses in the human body![2] We are more in rhythm than out of it. In fact, rhythm is what makes us alive. Our "job" is to let it out. I once read in a cookbook, "Don't let the fact that you don't have a soufflé dish stop you from making a soufflé."3 If you haven't got a drum, don't let that stop you. It's actually a good idea to experiment for a while until you find the kind of instrument that suits you best. There are many different kinds of drums and even more ways to play them. We'll get into searching for your drum in the chapter called "The Care and Feeding of Drums." But be careful: you might discover there is no such thing as "too many drums."

Just as rhythm is within and around us, we can turn many objects into rhythm instruments. Plastic bottles are great; big water containers and buckets can easily become drums; little pill bottles containing a few beads or beans make dandy rattles. Experiment with hands and sticks. I drum on the steering wheel with my hands at stoplights and keep a pair of drumsticks in the car to drum on the dashboard in time to the radio (when someone else is driving!). Wooden cabinets often have a very satisfying, deep voice.4 I've even used the body of my guitar as a hand drum.

Find music that moves you, either a recording or something you can sing (even if it's just in your head), and clap, tap, dance, sway. Let your rhythmic responses be like conversations. Experiment with simple and complex relationships in the music you hear. Listen for the songs and natural rhythms inside you and let *your* drummer out.

AND–A ONE, AND–A TWO
You may want to record this section for yourself, so you can feel free to move and still follow along.

Go for a walk, if that works for you, or simply rock from side to side where you are sitting, rocking at an easy, comfortable, regular pace: *back and forth and back and forth and back and forth*. Feel the simple rhythm? Say it silently to yourself or aloud, *"back and forth and back and forth,"* until it becomes automatic, like your body is repeating the words on its own. Keep the pulse as regular as you can, like a big pendulum swinging, "tick-tock-tick-tock." Now raise your hands in front of you and clap each *tick* and *tock* on your legs, alternating hands with each beat, *tick-tock-tick-tock*. Each *tick* and *tock* is a "beat."

Keep walking or rocking with that same regularity—each clap, step, or sway is in time with a *tick* or *tock*, *tick-tock-tick-tock*—but say "tick-and-tock-and-tick-and-tock." See how each "and" occupies the space in between the beats? That space is called the *"offbeat"*—*tick*-**and**-*tock*-**and**-*tick*-**and**-*tock*.

Okay, now go back to *tick-tock-tick-tock*, letting the steady rhythm carry you as if you were on a nice, long journey through a beautiful countryside with all the time in the world— *tick-tock-tick-tock*. Think of a big clock, the old-fashioned kind with hands that go around. Put *tick* where the number nine would go, and *tock* over at three o'clock. This is called a *rhythm cycle*: unlike a *line* of words...

"tick-tock-tick-tock"

...a cycle goes around and around without stopping. Each *tick* leads to another *tock*.

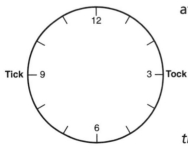

RHYTHM CYCLE

You can make a rhythmic cycle simple or complex, with as many beats per cycle as you like. In the chapter "Types of Drumming" we'll spend more time discussing rhythmic cycles. For now, is your body still going *tick-tock-tick-tock*? Great. When you make one full cycle and come back to where you started, that first beat is called the *downbeat*. In the two-beat cycle shown above, the downbeat is *tick*:

Tick-tock-**Tick**-tock-**Tick**-tock-**Tick**-tock

A four-beat cycle would sound like…

Tick-tock-tick-tock-**Tick**-tock-tick-tock

A three-beat cycle is a little trickier, since three is an odd number…

Tick-tock-tick-**Tock**-tick-tock-**Tick**-tock-tick

The emphasis changes, depending on how many beats per cycle, but good old *tick-tock-tick-tock* just keeps moving along in a steady, even pulsation.

The different rhythms—two, three, four, and so on—each have different qualities or moods associated with them, inherent in their structure. Elements like *tempo* (speed), and how the beats and offbeats within a cycle are accented or kept silent, also affect the flavor of a particular rhythm. A lullaby isn't soothing just because it is sung softly; a waltz isn't romantic just because of the lyrics or musical lines. A slow three-beat tends to bring our bodies into an elongated, rocking rhythm: **Tick**-*tock-tick-***Tock**-*tick-tock-***Tick**-*tock-tick*. A two-beat cycle goes by so quickly that it's no surprise a polka has such bounce. The longer four-beat cycle tends to have a more driving quality, like a march—or rock and roll. You can also combine the smaller two, three, and four-beat cycles into more complex rhythms like five, seven, nine, and so on (for example, a five-beat cycle could be sounded out, "**Tick**-tock-tick-tock-tick, **Tock**-tick-tock-tick-tock," 2 + 3 = 5).

Are you still going *tick-tock-tick-tock*? Never mind. And don't worry if you didn't get all this stuff about the flavors of different rhythmic cycles. The point is to start feeling the rhythms around you: in the music you hear, that dripping faucet, your own heartbeat. Start playing with rhythms, dancing to them, drumming with them. Find ways of interacting with the rhythms in your life. Experiment with sound and silence, beat and offbeat, until they become familiar toys you can play with in your imagination—and with your friends.

DRUMMING 101

Using Your Hands

Assume for the moment that you have a frame drum: an ancient style of drum that looks like a tambourine without the jangles, found all over the world. Frame or "hoop" drums are played with the hands, or with a single- or double-headed drumstick. For now, just use your hands.

Find a way to hold the drum comfortably in one hand. If you have a Native American style drum, it will have thongs across the back like a spider web so you can curl your fingers

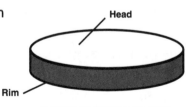

A SIMPLE DRUM FRAME

through the thongs. You may want to wrap a piece of cloth or deerskin around the rawhide to make it more comfortable.

Some drum makers design or use a padded handgrip (see All-One-Tribe in the Resources section at the back of this book—they have patented a very comfortable design). If you have a bodhrán (Celtic style hoop drum), it may have wooden cross members to stabilize the frame. You can grasp those as you would the thongs of the Native American drum. A Middle Eastern frame-drum (tar) typically does not have either wood or rawhide across the back, but may have a thumb-sized hole in the rim to give you something to grasp.[5]

Once you have found a comfortable way to hold the drum, experiment with your free hand to discover what kinds of sounds you can make. Notice how the tonal quality and resonance change, depending on how you play the drum. You can also experiment on any resonant surface—even this book—if you don't have a drum yet. A light tap with your fingertips will produce a very different sound than, say, a firm thump with the heel of your hand, especially if you stay in contact with the drumhead instead of bouncing. Experiment with alternating the two sounds; "tap" a light bounce, then land like a frog on a lily pad, "thump," and rest for a moment before hopping again: *tap-thump*, *tap-thump*, *tap-thump*, *tap-thump*. Can you imitate the rhythm of your heartbeat using the *tap-thump* combination? Would it sound more like your heart if you went *thump-tap*, instead?

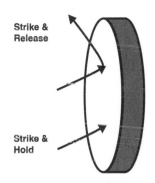

Strike & Release

Strike & Hold

CREATING DIFFERENT SOUNDS

Remember the classic gesture of boredom, "drumming your fingers" on a table? See what happens if you do that on the drum. How rapid a sequence of beats can you make? Try to imitate the sound of a galloping horse with your fingers: brrump-brrump-brrump-brrump. Now hold up your hand as if it were in a mitten: fingers together, thumb off by itself. In this position you have four different things you can do with your hand: tap with your thumb, slap with your fingers all together, thump with the heel of your hand, and clap with your whole hand. Notice the different qualities of sound you get with a clap-release, a clap-hold, and a variation of the clap-hold I call "the spider" (landing with all your fingertips spread, as a spider would land on its "feet"). Hold your hand near the surface of the drum and rotate lightly on the axis that runs from your index finger to elbow, fluttering back and forth between your thumb and fingers on the drum. Can you make a circus drum-roll this way?

THE "MITTEN" POSITION

You will also get different qualities of sound depending on the part of the drum's head you play. In general, the center of the drum will be deeper— more of a "boom." As you get closer to the edge, you will get a progressively more bell-like ringing tone. Also, the outer part of the head will tend to give a crisper sound and the center will probably sound more muffled, even if it is louder. If your drum is getting "flat" (see "The Care and Feeding of Drums"), you will get better sound playing out near the edge and be kinder to the drum, too.

Here's a tricky move: snap your fingers and watch what happens. Your thumb holds and then releases one finger like a latch. When that finger is released, it comes down with considerable force. If you rest the side of your hand on the edge of the drum in just the right position, that finger can glance off the very edge of the head, producing an intense, bright "bing." It may take a while to get the hang of it, but that *bing* is a nice bit of punctuation to add to your rhythmic vocabulary. You can make a similar sound by flicking your finger diagonally across the surface (as if you were flicking a crumb).

Ring

Boom

DIFFERENT QUALITIES OF SOUNDS

One last sound deserves a place in your repertoire: silence. A well-placed *rest* can be just as dynamic as any "hot licks" you may learn—providing accent, emphasis, and variation. Remember, rhythm does not stop just because there is no sound. Beethoven was innovative in his day, partly because of his use of silence. The first "sound" in his *Fifth Symphony* is a silent downbeat followed by three short pulsations in the two-beat cycle. It is offset by one long booming note that fills the whole next two-beat cycle: "**(Rest)**-ba-ba-ba, **Bom**, **(Rest)**-ba-ba-ba, **Bom**…" Keep the rhythm going inside you and let your drumbeats weave around it like a dance partner. Silence can act like a springboard for the sound that follows it.

You may be working with something other than a frame drum, such as a *conga, dhoumbek, djembe*, or *ashiko*. As you get more comfortable with yourself as a drummer, you may discover that a particular kind of drum is more suited to your body or personal expression. For beginners, the main differences are how the drum is held, whether it is traditionally played with sticks or hands, and what kind of voice it has. Regardless of the kind of drum you start with, you can still experiment with all the different hand moves and see what happens. If you have a *dhoumbek* (a lap-sized drum from the Middle East), try laying the drum on its side and playing it with both hands. You will have to reach around the body of the drum with one arm, but it will give your hands different approaches on the drum. This way, you can have the fun of putting one hand into the throat of the drum to change the tonal quality and make an almost bubbling sound. The *dhoumbek* gets its name from the sounds it makes: *dhoum* in the center, and *bek* on the edge.

DHOUMBEK

This may be a good time to stop reading for a while and just experiment with your new drumming repertoire. Think back on the different ways to make sounds that we've discussed.

- tap with your thumb
- slap with your fingers all together
- thump with the heel of your hand

- clap with your whole hand
- snap the edge

 You can give each of these sounds a name that has meaning for you (like *tap* and *thump*). Then try playing with rhythmic patterns by mixing all the sounds together—like *thump-tap-froggie-froggie, thump-tap-froggie-froggie*—can you hear it? Or, play along with some recorded music that inspires the drummer in you.

Using a Mallet

Choosing a Mallet—A mallet is a padded drumstick. It gives a softer sound than the wooden sticks typically used to play a snare drum (European tradition), or the tschehs and bachi sticks used in Korean and Japanese drumming. Since

WOODEN DRUMSTICKS

it is padded, a mallet is also gentler on both drums and ears, especially for beginners. In this book, we are only going to work with padded sticks. The thickness of a mallet's padding and handle are a matter of personal preference, but are also dependent on the size of drum you are playing. Some people like a lightweight mallet, while others prefer something more substantial. When selecting a drumstick, test how it feels in your hand and how it sounds on the drum you will be playing.

 Ergonomics—Listen to your body as you listen to your drum. When learning something new, it's challenging to pay attention to everything at once. How you hold your drumstick will

**SOFT-HEADED
DRUM MALLET**

affect the sound of your drumming and, over time, it will also affect how you feel. By forming good habits in the beginning, you will have a better long-term experience. Stay loose and relaxed. Take stretch breaks. Notice how your body feels and, if something is uncomfortable, make the necessary adjustments. Remember to breathe and let your whole body enjoy drumming.

I used to be a carpenter. It took me a while to realize that I didn't need much force to play a drum. So I came up with this mantra to remind myself:

This is not a hammer,

This is not a nail...

Whatever helps. You will produce more pleasing sounds if you hold your sticks lightly and let gravity do most of the work. Save those big, booming sounds for accent. You and your drum will last longer, and, if you are playing in a group, it will be easier for you to hear what the others are playing, too.

There's no need to clutch your stick. A light hand does fine most of the time. Try this: Hold your hand "palm up," as if someone was about to drop a set of keys into it. Now lay a drumstick across your palm so that the stick can rest there by its own balance with the padded end extending out in the direction of your thumb. Wrap your index finger across the stick so that your finger touches the pad of your thumb. Next, wrap the rest of your fingers around the stick, but loosely enough so that only your index finger is holding the stick. Use the stick as if you were playing an invisible drum and see how lightly you can hold the drumstick without dropping it. Now, try playing on the drum as easily as you "played" the air. Another thing to watch is the position of your thumb. Keep it wrapped around the drumstick, not parallel to it!

Drumming with a Mallet—Think back to all the different ways of playing a drum with your hands. With a mallet you can also do many different things:

- play the center or the edge
- strike and release
- drum roll
- vary the force
- tap the drum rim with the handle of your stick

If your drum is freestanding or strapped to your body, you can experiment with using a stick in each hand or playing with one stick and one hand. You may want to experiment with walking or even dancing while you drum.

Let your whole body move. Instead of working from the wrist or elbow, let your whole arm carry the drumstick in a loose, easy stroke. Shake out any tension you notice in your body and relax into what you are doing. Hold your drum and drumstick lightly. Hold yourself lightly, too.

Mental images you hold while drumming will also have an effect on the way it sounds. For example, some traditions teach us to drum as though your stroke were passing right through the drum, instead of bouncing off of it. Others say to lift the sound out of the drum, as if your hands or sticks were ladling some magic sound-soup from a bowl or cauldron. Experiment with your own imagination; feel and listen to the effect that different mental images have on the music you make. Maybe you have an image of your own that best suits your own, unique spirit.

PAYING ATTENTION

The Native American *métis* teacher Brooke Medicine Eagle teaches about the *Three Attentions:*

- *First Attention:* the body
- *Second Attention:* internal or external task-at-hand
- Third Attention: holiness, holding the entire circle of life in awareness[6]

By learning to stay aware of these Three Attentions, we develop proficiency and grace in our endeavors. It is as if we have three leads connecting us to our purpose—like the reins guiding a team of horses. It also gives us three different focal lengths in the zoom lens of our mind's eye:

1. What am I doing?
2. How am I doing what I am doing?
3. How does what I am doing fit into what is happening around me?

In sacred drumming—either alone or in a group—your First Attention is to the mechanics: your posture, how you hold the drum and drumsticks, how you connect the drum and drumstick to produce different sounds. The Second Attention is to the relationship between the drummer's heart/mind and the drumming dedication—staying connected to the reason for drumming—keep the mental focus from leaping back and forth to another time, place, or agenda (we'll talk more about this in *The Basic Elements of Ceremony*). The Third Attention is to the circle—keeping a harmonious balance between expressing your own uniqueness and reinforcing the unity of the whole. Even though you may be drumming alone, you are nonetheless part of the Great Circle of all living things. Harmony only comes when we each know and play our own part. If we are all doing exactly the same thing, it is "unison." If we stay in unison for too long, it becomes regimented and dull. Harmony takes courage, confidence, and awareness of the whole.

Sacred drumming is a spiritual practice focusing attention, intention, body/mind, and spirit/feeling. May the care and creativity you bring to your drumming be a source of joy and growth for you and all of those you meet in the Great Circle of life.

CHAPTER 2

WHY DROUM?

The journey into rhythm begins with a pulsation. It begins by going into that place deep inside yourself and listening—not to external noises—but to the pulses within your own body. What do you hear? Your breath moving back and forth through nostrils, windpipe, and lungs, the sound of your heartbeat.

As you sit very, very still, feel the subtle movement in your body, perhaps in response to your heartbeat or breathing. Follow the movement by allowing it to grow and become more prominent and then gradually recede into the tiniest micro-movement, discernable only to yourself. Focus your attention on that rhythm. Don't try to name it or analyze it. Just let it be there; let it fill the space of your mind with pulsation, as if you were the ocean and had nothing to do but roll with your own tide.

This is the beginning of rhythm; more ancient than any musical tradition, as old as life itself. It is in everything from a heartbeat to the food chain, to the immense quadrille of planets around the sun, to the expansion and contraction from one Big Bang to the next. Drumming focuses our attention on the primal rhythms of life. It magnifies and expands those rhythms, playing with their depth and breadth, exploring the furthest reaches of their possibility, or celebrating their very simplicity.

So why drum together? Drumming is an efficient, non-verbal way to synchronize our energies. When two hearts are in close proximity to one another they tend to *entrain*, to find a common rhythm, to "beat as one." Work songs around the world have long been used as a way of helping a group of people function together as a team: drums have led warriors into battle, shamans to other realities, dancers into ecstatic trance.

Percussion of one sort or another has been part of the human experience for as long as we have existed. When we walk we express rhythm. We rock our babies to sleep, perhaps humming little spontaneous melodies or lullabies we heard as children, patting them softly in time with our rocking and singing. Repetitive tasks like digging, planting, carving, winnowing, weaving, and kneading dough, all naturally fall into rhythmic patterns which sometimes develop into songs. So rhythm is not something we have to *try* to learn, it has accompanied us in even the most mundane activities for centuries. Modern urban life has diminished the daily experience of these rhythms, replacing them with less harmonious or even frenetic pulses and paces. But the natural rhythm is in us like a computer program that just needs to be started—all the more reason for making a conscious choice to re-equilibrate our lives and re-awaken our senses through drumming.

APPROACHES TO RHYTHM

We humans are such verbal creatures. We use words and images to describe music in order to remember and pass along what we hear or imagine, or to explain and analyze its characteristics. For years I described myself as a "seat of the pants" musician (did you ever hear the expression, "flying by the seat of the pants?"). If I heard a song, chances were I could pick it out on the piano or guitar or hop into a jam session with other musicians. But the process of trying to translate written music, with its notes lying lifeless on a page, into something alive that moved through me—something I could express from my soul—was a daunting task. I'm still not very good at it. But over the years I have come to appreciate being able to read music because it increases my understanding of musical forms and makes it possible for me to perform with other musicians in complex compositions, for example by singing in a choir.

There are many different doorways into the world of rhythm. In this chapter we'll explore a few of them. If the mere mention of music theory is enough to make your mind go into vapor lock, don't worry. You can skim over anything that doesn't work for you and still have a good time drumming (meet me in a few pages at the heading, "Free Drumming"). Maybe some day you'll want to come back and take another look. On the other hand, this may help to put things into perspective.

How rhythm is expressed, even perceived, is a reflection of culture and learning. We will look at three different ways of describing rhythm: as a line, a circle, and a spiral.

To a classically trained musician of the European tradition, rhythm is like a yardstick upon which music is measured out. In fact, a single revolution of a rhythm cycle is called a measure. In this way, a piece of music can be written and repeated with great predictability. Listen to several different musicians play The Goldberg Variations (for solo keyboard) and you will soon recognize the music, reproduced with precision from the notations J. S. Bach first wrote down some three hundred years ago. Rhythm in this context may be almost invisible; yet it is the organizing structure upon which the musical composition is constructed, like the gridlines on a spreadsheet.[1] Without rhythm, who would know how those notes were to be played?

Prior to the late nineteenth century, percussion instruments were used sparingly if at all in the concert halls of Europe. Then, avant-garde composers, like Stravinsky and Bartók, began to experiment with the dynamic potential of percussion. Actual percussion ensembles did not appear until the twentieth century with more innovative composers (most notably Edgard Varèse, John Cage, Lou Harrison, and Henry Cowell).[2] The folk music of Europe, the British Isles, and North America traditionally gave percussion instruments more authority (as did the military). As Afro-derivative and European folk traditions merged in North America during the twentieth century, percussion instruments again became standard equipment in contemporary music—popular, classical, or otherwise. Where would jazz, rhythm and blues, or rock and roll music be without a drummer?

But even today, underlying the European-based musical tradition, there is still a linear approach to rhythm, expressed in *signature*, with *bars* and *measures* and *meter*. Whether you're reading Beethoven or Baez or the Beatles, the notes are written on a *staff* and divided into *measures*. And, whether expressed in thundering kettle drums, or the silent, subtle toe-tapping of a bassoon player, waiting to recall a *leitmotif* for a few measures, rhythm provides the structure for it all. There are times when notes are written on a staff without being divided into measures, but the very lack of rhythmic notation expresses the composer's desire for a loose, lyrical style giving greater interpretive latitude to the performer.

II. COUNTERDANCE IN THE SPRING

Take a look at this illustration. The composer is Lou Harrison, one of the musical magicians of the twentieth century.[3] Each group of five lines is called a staff and expresses the musical instructions for (in this case) one musician. The three staffs are linked together into a system, which means the three musical lines are played simultaneously. See the numbers written in each staff that look almost like fractions? The top one indicates how many beats per measure (rhythmic cycle) and the bottom number tells what kind of note receives a beat (whole note, half, quarter, etc.). In this case the eighth notes (they're the ones with one flag on the stem) get a whole beat. Just like fractions, a whole note would count the same as eight eighth notes. The little marks resembling a percent symbol are eighth rests (silent beats). There are three percussionists. The first one to start plays two gongs, the second, two tortoise shells, and the third, two drums. Notice that the gong player has a five-beat rhythmic cycle, but the tortoise shell player has a three-beat cycle and the drummer, four beats. So they each have down-beats at different times. The drummer ("Percussion 3") doesn't even start playing until the beginning of the second system (see the rests). At the end of the second system, they all meet together on the same downbeat, and continue together to a count of five. Wild. It would be nearly impossible to give this kind of instructions if you couldn't write it down!

So we have rhythm as a linear measuring tool.

Rhythm can also be expressed as a cycle made of a group of rhythmic elements. The cycle has a beginning point and internal structure which leads back around to that same beginning point, over and over again. The rhythmic cycle provides a structure upon which can be superimposed dance, singing, even other rhythms. Tying the cycle together is a regular return to the *downbeat*. The *downbeat* is the point of agreement for everything that is added to a rhythm cycle, however simple or complex that cycle may be. Let's describe a four-beat cycle by saying:

Boom-chukka-chukka-chukka

"Boom" is the *downbeat* and "chukka-chukka-chukka" is the internal structure of the cycle. Sometimes several different internal structures are played at the same time, meeting briefly again and again on the downbeat. This is rhythm as cycle—a "pie" that can be divided in countless different ways but always circles back around within a defined structure.

Describing rhythm as a cycle comes from oral traditions which may be very structured and complex, even if they are not written down. Whole compositions can be expressed in words mapping the face of a drum, the kind or intensity of a stroke, a series of rhythm cycles. If we agree that "Boom" is a loud, forceful slap in the center of the drum, and "chukka" means "tap two fingers lightly in a one-two dance on the rim," you see how it can be done. With centuries of tradition to develop a system, imagine how sophisticated the information packed into each syllable could become.

So now we have rhythm as yardstick, and rhythm as cycle. Both systems provide structures that make it possible to create beautiful and intricate music: everything from symphonies, bluegrass, and jazz, to samba, taiko, African-based rhythms, rock and roll, you name it!

But there is another way to approach rhythm and that is as a spiral leading into unknown territories, singing for the personal unconscious, or expressing the collective spirit of a group. This is free drumming: immediate and available to everyone from expert musician to complete novice alike.

Free drumming is non-literate and unplanned, but not without structure. However, the structure is not music describing rhythmical patterns. It is a structure of *intent*. The sound is less important than the experience; the outcome less important than the journey. Consider for a moment the concept of musical outcome. The idea of performance without an audience is reminiscent of the question of a tree falling in the forest with no one to hear. Is this still a performance? In the case of free drumming, the audience (should there be one at all) is a mere spectator at an internal event. Far more value is placed on the experience of the drummer(s). Structure, such as it is, is about communication between the drummer and her/his own unconscious and between all the members of the drumming circle. Free drumming, then, is about non-verbal communication. Its spiral structure is the map of a conversation—beginning as a cycle, but spinning out into a rhythmic adventure.

FREE DRUMMING

It can be argued that, of all ways of drumming, free drumming has the longest history and is the most widespread throughout the world. Whether the setting is structured or informal, people are drawn to creating rhythms together, carrying on non-verbal rhythmic conversations, sharing emotions and experiences, mirroring the world around them, and expressing their own creativity. In free drumming, the circle manifests the group energy: every session is unique, a journey into the psyche of each individual and simultaneously a reflection of the collective unconscious of the group. Quite the opposite of performance drumming, this is drumming which is focused inward; the role of drummer and drummed all but merge and the drum seems to take on a life of its own.

Although knowledge of rhythmic patterns and technique can be very useful in a performance, it can actually get in the way of free drumming. The free drummer who can show up without a preconceived idea of form, content, or destination may actually be more able to contact the fresh inner territory available in *beginner's mind*. For this is clearly *not* about performance, but about journey for journey's sake, inter- (or *inner-*) personal communication as its own reward.

An experienced group of free drummers may talk very little about a session, either before or after, since it is often difficult, even ludicrous, to verbalize what happens, especially when the communication is very deep. More than once I have had the experience of recording a particularly awesome drumming session, only to discover later that what happened was more about connection than it was about musicality. As the saying goes, "you had to have been there." The product is the *direct experience of drumming together.*

When free drumming in a group, it is very typical for a pattern to emerge something like this: someone will start a rhythm and other drummers will join in as they feel ready. Depending on their experience with drumming and with each other, drummers will play more or less "together," each one finding a comfortable place in the rhythmical pattern. Often there will be a period of struggle as individual drummers search for their particular expression within the whole. This may even border on cacophony. But, in my experience, if participants are willing to let go of the need to do it right, if they can evict that inner critic and persist, there will usually be a point when something shifts automatically and the group finds its natural rhythm, sliding almost effortlessly into sync.[4]

Years ago I was a member of an environmental education puppet troupe called *Puppets on the Path*. We developed our own characters, built our own puppets, wrote our own music. In defining the relationship between puppets and people, we discarded terms of ownership like "my puppet." Instead, we spoke of ourselves as the "talking-mouth person" of a particular character. The puppets seemed to have such distinct personalities that those of us who created and carried them felt, at times, as if the puppets had lives of their own, which we humans simply supported.

Nowadays I often experience "my" drums in much the same way; that, if I can keep my ego sufficiently out of the way, the drums themselves will speak through me. Each instrument resonates with a different part of my self. Or, more accurately, different parts of *me* resonate with particular drums. However you choose to interpret it, I urge you to experiment with letting your conscious mind—your preconceived ideas of *how things are supposed to be*—drop as far into the background as possible and let the drum speak for you and through you.

Don't get the idea that you need companions to free drum, rewarding as that can be. A drum is also a very personal tool. You may not even want to share it with other people. In fact, among drummers, there is an important point of etiquette: Ask permission before touching someone else's instruments. Drumming alone can also be a deep experience. In "Basic Elements of Ceremony" we'll look at steps you can take to create a sacred space for drumming alone or in a group, ways of preparing your mental and physical environment.

TYPES OF DRUMMING

In this discussion, our focus is not on style or technique but on *intention*. The determining factor is the drummer's relationship with the listener or audience, if such a relationship exists at all. These distinctions aren't carved in stone; any explicit reason for drumming may carry with it, by design or surprise, other purposes as well. But it is often useful to separate concepts for better understanding, only to watch them later merge into a larger picture. Underlying any obvious reason for drumming is a primal connection with rhythm calling the drummer to play. For our purposes, let's consider three different types of drumming: Performance, Anchor, and Trance/Unitive.

Performance Drumming

Whether the knowledge is passed on through oral or written tradition, performance drumming follows a form, reproducing (loosely or precisely) a previously determined rhythmic structure. It is something rehearsed and prepared for delivery to an audience. That audience may be on their feet and dancing in time to the rhythm, or quietly experiencing a performance, but there is a defined relationship of giver (percussionist) and recipient (audience, dancers, etc.).

Anchor Drumming

As an anchor, the drummer(s) provide support for spiritual work, whether it is ceremony, ritual dance, teaching, story-telling, or shamanic journey. Until the modern era, it would have been nearly impossible to find a culture in which this kind of drumming did not exist. Its goal is to maintain an environment of sacred space or to coordinate a group's energy around a particular task (such as agriculture or construction). In ceremony, the drum's capacity to synchronize group energy is useful, as is drumming to establish, perpetuate, or shift a mood. The anchor drummer has a clearly defined task and, like the performance drummer, must stay present and aware. Anchor drumming holds the energy for the participant(s), acting as focal point, grounding, vehicle, or background.

The example of a ceremonial camp described in the Introduction, where group drumming was maintained for days, epitomizes the use of percussion to synchronize and ground group energy. The community danced, ate, slept, worked, prayed, and met in council to the ever-present heartbeat of the great Mother Drum. Even after the gathering was officially over and the drumming ceased, many people remarked that they continued to hear the heartbeat drumming for days.

Brooke Medicine Eagle uses anchor drumming effectively in her teaching format, by enlisting drummers to maintain a soft but constant heartbeat as she talks, tells stories, and guides meditation, ceremony, and shamanic journey. When I drum for Brooke, participants often remark that the drumming helps her teachings penetrate their consciousness in deep ways, that it holds their attention, and helps build group cohe-siveness. By integrating periods of circle dancing and singing—also supported by drumming—into the format, her teaching moves beyond a mind-centered delivery of information to a direct experience of heart-centered body wisdom.

All over North America, large community drums and hand drums are still used extensively in ceremonies among the many diverse cultures of Native American and First Nations peoples. Community drums are also used in more recent traditions which have evolved from indigenous cultures of the Western Hemisphere and Africa. Drumming, singing, and dancing provide important methods for perpetuating and enhancing cultural identity, knowledge, and traditions.

The Dances of Universal Peace, or "Sufi Dancing" as it is commonly called, is an example of sacred dance. Sufi Dancing is a practice in which the participants simultaneously sing sacred text and join in circle dancing. Usually one or more musicians in the center of the circle provide a rhythmic container for the singing and dancing. Often a *doumbek* (Middle Eastern, hourglass-shaped drum) is played to show respect for the culture from which Sufism emerged.

The musicians are responsible for paying close attention to, and reflecting back, the instructions of the dance leader, maintaining rhythm and tempo, and being in sync with the natural ebb and flow of volume and intensity. Although Sufi Dancing is by design a trance-inducing practice, it is the musician's responsibility to maintain a balance between being aware of the group's energy and staying present for the leader's signals.

"For the shaman, the drum is not so much a musical in-strument as a vehicle for transportation."[5] Many shamanic tra-ditions depend upon some kind of repetitive percussion to induce altered states of consciousness. The shaman may drum or use a rattle in spirit dancing, journey preparation, or in the actual journey.

The role of a shaman's drummer is to stay present, to maintain a steady drum beat so that the one who is making the journey has a solid foundation, to provide a dependable vehicle, and a clear focal point for re-entry. The shaman's drummer must be fully involved without going into trance. She or he is the shaman's servant, giving a clear point of departure and return. Like a performer, the shaman's drummer has a clearly defined relationship with the receiver (in this case, shaman rather than audience); yet, quite the opposite of the performer, the anchor drummer's role is to be—in a sense—in-visible, to provide the container without filling it.

Trance/Unitive Drumming

Gathered around a single dominant rhythm, we tend to en-train in a common pulse. Imagine how much more immediate and profound this experience can be if a group consciously en-gages their intention and attention on connecting as a group by drumming together! Trance/unitive drumming, like anchor drumming, provides a context for participants to support one another in inner work, ceremony, celebration, and community building. The drummer(s) do not remain apart, but use their own drumming as a gateway into states of trance. Anchor drumming supports the group; in trance/unitive drumming, the drummers *are* the group, so their experience can leap from a personal to *transpersonal* dimension.

Trance/unitive ("circle") drumming can be found world-wide. In traditional cultures, rhythms, ceremonies, and protocol are often highly structured and precisely followed. Modern drum circles often have a spontaneous, flowing style. Although markedly different, both approaches can produce amazing results. Ask yourself what you want and need from a drum circle. Perhaps just getting together to jam with friends is enough. But maybe there is something tugging you in the direction of a more explicitly spiritual experience. If so, the chapter on "The Basic Elements of Ceremony" will help you discover ways to integrate drumming into an already existing practice, or imagine something new for yourself.

Merging

The distinctions between performance, anchor, and trance/unitive drumming are not as cut and dried as one might think. Who's to say whether a performance is trance producing, or if a trance drummer is performing?

Western cultures have enjoyed a recent renaissance in drumming, including the re-appearance of drums in medical, spiritual, and educational settings. Drummers who started out as performers have discovered spiritual dimensions of rhythm and their careers have been transformed in the process:

- Layne Redmond[6] (who performed for years with Glen Velez) and her Mob of Angels have been "performing" earth-based ceremonies for audiences for nearly a decade.

- Mickey Hart (The Grateful Dead) has co-authored two books[7] on drumming and, with Dr. Oliver Sacks, formed The Rhythm For Life Foundation to support the use of rhythm in medical, educational, and community-based settings.[8]

- Heidrun Hoffmann has founded DiRRiD ("Dance in Rhythm-Rhythm in Dance"),[9] a new model for understanding and teaching rhythm, based on the TaKeTiNa approach developed by Reinhard Flatischler.[10]

- Taiko (Japanese tradition) groups are springing up in communities across the United States, in response to the growing enthusiasm for this style of drumming, largely as a result of the Kodo Drummers of Sado Island, Japan, who have introduced taiko to the world community through "concert" tours.

- Babatunde Olatunji, a master percussionist from Nigeria, tours extensively with his ensemble, Drums of Passion, spreading the inspiration of his tradition to drummers and dancers who often form their own communities in response to the experience.

"Life itself is a movement towards the soul,"[11] and drums speak for the soul. We are instinctively drawn to drumming as a means for finding our way back to wholeness, to an activation of our spiritual dimensions. For some, that can mean the discipline of drum lessons, the good fortune of finding an inspiring teacher, or the blessing of an equally dedicated circle of fellow drumming students. But, for many of us, the immediacy of free drumming can offer a context in which to begin the process of exploring new aspects of our own possibilities; to explore rhythm in ways both personal and communal, and to start drumming today.

I lived for a time in an old trailer on top of a mountain, with no job, no car, and no money. I had a soulful drum and a great view of the sunrise. In retrospect, it sounds romantic, but at the time I thought my life was in a shambles. In order to escape the panic attacks I often wakened to, I got into the habit of crawling out of bed when my eyes were still barely open, picking up my drum, and going to greet the sunrise.

I danced and sang whatever came to mind, drummed and rattled alone on the mountaintop. I imagined that the rattle was a sort of psychic scrub brush to cleanse and fluff my aura, and that the drum was my conduit to the heartbeat of the Earth herself. Though healers throughout time have used these simple tools, I had no formal training, only instinct telling me this was what I needed. Laughing, crying, wailing, sighing, the drum and rattle became the life raft and paddle to carry me to a new state of wellness and a relationship with my own soul, which was beyond words.

CHAPTER 3

THE CARE AND FEEDING OF DRUMS

FINDING A DRUM OF YOUR OWN

Like people, drums come in many different shapes and sizes. Some have huge, resonant voices, others seem to murmur. Some are exquisitely decorated and ornate, others are plain, even funky. Some drums are traditionally played with the hands, others with sticks. Shopping for a drum can feel a little like attending a singles function—you dance with one partner after another, looking for someone with whom you have a mutual understanding and resonance.

Hopefully, you will be able to try out many different drums before you choose one for yourself. If you have the good fortune to know other drummers, or to visit a store where drums are sold, you can have some hands-on experience and find out what style of drumming appeals to you. There are wonderful teaching tools available as well—books, video and audio cassettes—to help you explore different styles of drums and drumming (see Resources).

Once you have decided what kind of drum you are looking for, you can start searching for just the right one. In addition to music stores, you can sometimes find drums in bookshops that specialize in Native American or New Age titles. If all else fails, you can resort to mail order catalogs or online drum sellers, though it is better to meet a drum face to face if possible. Here are some things to watch for when you are shopping for a drum.

Construction

You want a drum that will last for a long time. It can be very distressing to watch your beloved companion crack and tear, so be sure to examine your prospects carefully. Native American-style frame drums have become very popular, partly because they are light and portable. New Age stores and catalogs often carry these drums, which may be painted with shamanic themes. I have two such drums for different climates. One is especially for the foggy coastal mountains of California where I live. The other was my first drum, purchased during a pivotal summer in Montana. She's a soulful old drum who has accompanied me on many adventures and taught me a great deal about taking care of a drum. Some of her thongs run through holes that were punched much too close to the edge of the hide, making the hide vulnerable to tearing. The skin is of inconsistent thickness. The way the thongs are knotted in the back is miserably uncomfortable, so I've padded it with an old bandanna. She's temperamental and likes hot, dry weather so I can rarely

BACK VIEW OF AN OLD FRAME DRUM

even play her unless I'm in a climate like Arizona's. And yet, I love this drum. When conditions are just right, she has a clear, bell-like voice. But I worry and fuss, blow dry and baby her to get that sound. The "fog drum" was made for my home climate so it takes a long and dreary winter to make that drum go flat.

Before buying a drum, examine the head carefully. Look for thin spots in the skin and be sure it rolls cleanly over the rim of the drum without bumps or dips or torn spots. Tap lightly and forcefully to be sure you get a clean sound without any buzz or snare. Not all drum heads are fastened with thongs. Some are tacked or glued and others are held by a combination of rings, ropes, or screws—designs that make them tunable. There are definite advantages to this type of design, especially if your drum is going to be subjected to major atmospheric fluctuations because of travel or a change-able climate.

Examine how the head is attached to the body of the drum. Make sure it is fastened securely, and rolls smoothly over the edge of the rim. If there are holes punched in the hide for tacks or thongs, make sure the holes are far enough away from the edge of the skin to avoid tearing. There are manufacturers (Remo is the most famous) who make drums from synthetic materials. I used to turn up my nose at the idea, but they have remarkable tone quality and competitive prices. Step back and think about what you want from a drum. A sturdy, inexpensive Mylar drum that is ready to play rain or shine, day or night, that you don't feel anxious about loaning to a kid or stuffing in a backpack, might be just the thing.

The body will probably be wooden, ceramic, or metal. In any case, look it over for cracks, dents, loose or missing machinery, and flimsy or broken thongs or ropes. Make sure the drum fits your body well. A glamorous but unwieldy drum loses its appeal if it is too heavy, gives you blisters, or is no fun to play. If possible, hang out at the drum seller's and play the drum for a while. Selecting a drum is a little like trying on shoes—you need a good fit.

How Can You Tell When a Drum Sounds Right?

When a drum is singing, it has an almost bell-like ring that floats over the "boom" sound you first notice. I call it the "angel voices" of a drum. To make angel voices, a head needs to be tight, but not too tight. As you get better acquainted with the way different drums sound, your ears will become more sensitive to the messages a drum tells you about how it is feeling. If you have a tunable drum, learn how to loosen and tighten the head using the fasteners the drum has. Make any adjustments to the fasteners in a uniform way all around the circumference of the head to avoid unnecessary stress. If the head is mounted with sinews or tacks (in other words, not "tunable"), you will need to learn how to deal with atmospheric conditions (heat and moisture) to maintain proper tension.

TENSION

too loose	just right	too tight
low, flat, dead	rich, resonant "angels"	too high, tense, dry

SOUNDS

Speaking of stress, be careful when you take your drum traveling. Excessive heat or cold can do irreparable damage. If you must fly your drum as baggage, be sure to loosen the head if it is tunable, or use the techniques described below to keep the head "flat." I never (and I mean never) check a drum as baggage, though I know some drummers—especially touring professionals—who do. They have special containers and procedures to protect their equipment from the trauma of "life on the road." I always take my drum as carry-on luggage. The Mother Drum doesn't venture further from home than I'm willing to drive.

Blow Dryers and Plant Misters

Keep in mind that if a drum is too damp, the head will become too loose, and begin to sound relatively low-pitched and lack resonance (called "dead" or "flat"). When it sounds that way, do not play the drum until you have solved the problem. A skin under the proper tension actually repels a drumstick, but as the skin goes limp, it runs a greater risk of being torn or stretched. One way to tell the difference is by asking yourself what kind of word the drum is saying. If you could use a word that ends in "ing" (like "bing") the drum is not too loose. But if the word ends in an "h" (like "buh") or a "p" ("slap"), your drum probably needs some attention. Your hand or mallet should bounce as if the drum were a little trampoline.

MOISTURE CONTENT

TENSION

If your drum is not tunable, you will have to become a little more imaginative when your drum goes flat. You might be surprised how many drummers travel with a blow dryer, not for their hair, but for their drums. When drying out a drum, put your hand between the heat source and the drum as a test. If it's too hot for your hand, it's also too hot for the drum. Unless your drum has a synthetic head (in which case you won't need to dry it out, anyway) it's made of skin, just like your hand. Dry it out too quickly and it will become brittle and crisp, damaging the skin and the sound, and shortening the life of the drum. I've spent many sunny afternoons outside with my drums preparing them for an evening event and then wrapping them well to protect them against moisture. A nice, warm car can also do the trick—if it's not too hot!

Excessive dryness is even more life threatening to a drum than dampness. I remember being called to someone's room during a conference in Palm Springs in the middle of summer. She was near panic because the skin of her new drum was literally turning white—a sign of severe stress and dryness. We gently moistened it by stroking the surface and thongs with our wet hands until the skin finally relaxed and the sound returned to normal. For the rest of the conference she kept the drum in her hotel bathroom. A light spray with a plant mister would have been another way to gently ease the drum's distress. If you know you're going to be in hot, dry weather, plan to take one along. You can also put a sponge that has been squeezed fairly dry into an open plastic sandwich bag inside the drum, making sure the sponge is not touching the drum directly. Then put the drum in a plastic bag to hold in the sponge's moisture.

Think about where you are going to store the drum when it's not in use. I hang my old Montana drum on a wall near the fireplace to keep it relatively dry, and the "fog" drum on the other side of the room, so it doesn't get too dried out. Pick a safe spot for your drum, but where it's easy to reach, so you will be more tempted to play it often. This may sound like a lot of fuss and bother, but personally, I like relating to my drums in this intimate way. They all have names, personalities, and dedications. A few even have their own blanket and carrying case. Some—like the Mother Drum—are members of a community, so I go where the drum is called. Others are my personal vehicles for inner work, and I rarely put them into the hands of anyone else. Each drum carries stories with it: who made it, how I came to have it, adventures we've had, circles we've shared…

SPIRITUAL CONNECTION

Personal ritual objects take on a special place in our lives, serving us in several different ways. On a practical level, they are tools fulfilling a function. For example, a drum is a musical instrument for producing percussion. From a psychological point of view, ritual objects can be seen as useful self-hypnotic anchors by which we tune our consciousness to a particular frequency. A shamanic perspective might attribute an object with a specific supernatural energy, or see it as a line of communication with metaphysical realms. How you choose to relate to ritual objects is a matter of personal spiritual orientation. In discovering your own pathway toward sacred drumming, here are some things to consider.

Naming and Drum Dedication

Over the years, I have named my musical instruments. To play a guitar or a hand drum, one embraces it. The instrument becomes a counterpart, a companion on the journey of self-discovery and expression. It's easy to understand why love songs have been written to musical instruments.

To live in a sacred manner means to pay attention to where we are, where we come from, and where we are going. One way we do this is by expressing gratitude for all the help we receive along the way recognizing that we are part of a great web of life. Everyone and everything is interconnected, inter-affected, and mutually supporting. To hold a drum in a sacred manner, I must notice that other beings gave their lives in order for the instrument to come into my hands.

Some might say, "This wood or this hide was simply part of a large corporate harvest of animal and plant resources. There was nothing sacred about the process, nor was there any willingness on the part of the ones who made the sacrifice." In the process of re-weaving the torn fabric of our world, this is all the more reason to honor the spirit of the departed. We do not own the Earth or anything upon her, but live in relationship with everything. If we forget this simple truth, we fall out of balance with ourselves and our community.

I got my first drum the day I stepped out of the tipi after drumming until dawn. I was in heaven, and carried the drum with me everywhere I went. I drummed on the hilltop, drummed in the valley, drummed in the sweat lodge, drummed in the cave, drummed "in my sleep." I felt that I had achieved something important.

A group of us spent that summer "on the road." A few weeks later, we met again in Nevada, at Joy Lake, for another week of drumming and dancing with Brooke Medicine Eagle. There were many new drum carriers there, with all the blush and excitement of teenagers in puppy love, doting over and discussing our new drums. Brooke led us through a drum dedication ceremony that grounded and guided us toward an even deeper awareness of what it can mean to approach life in a sacred manner. I share this ceremony with you.[1]

When you have at last found your drum, take some time to be alone with it. Enter your own stillness and let the drum speak to you. If possible, let this be your first journey with your new drum (see "Meditations"). Try to give your rational mind and personality a vacation and focus your attention on the drum. Take three questions with you: Ask for your drum's name, dedication, and song.

Ritually cleanse the drum with incense smoke and a little water (a touch, not a bath!), removing any negative energy from the cutting of wood, killing of animals, others' handling the drum, and so on. Take some time to make offerings (tobacco for unity, cornmeal as spirit food) and prayers—for yourself, the drum, and All Our Relations. Return to the circle. When it is time, hold your drum up for all to see and call out its name and dedication on behalf of the drum. You might say something like, "My name is Open Hands, and I dedicate my life to invoking generosity and abundance." Paint or other decorations on the drum serve as reminders of this moment. If you are sharing the ritual with other new drums, go around the circle with each drum carrier speaking for her or his own drum. Then play four songs in celebration.

Dedicating a community drum, or Mother Drum, is rightly a community event. The ceremony for our Mother Drum, *Heart of Peace*, focused around twenty-four hours of continuous drumming. Visitors came and went all during that time, offering songs and dances, telling stories, and sleeping by the drum. When a second Mother Drum *Akasha* arrived, her drum carrier Raya organized a celebration in a local church and passed flyers around town.

Some traditions are very strict regarding drum protocol. There are rules about how to approach a drum, who drums, when and where to drum, proper offerings to make, and so on. As you deepen your relationship with drumming, these are questions to keep in mind and pursue. For me to present a patchwork of teachings from disparate practices would risk obscuring the intent of this book, which is to invite you to discover sacred drumming for yourself and integrate it with your own tradition.

The Personal Drum

By naming a drum and linking it with a specific purpose as we've discussed, the drum begins to take on more personal characteristics, which you can enhance with decorations that have particular meaning for you. You may also want to make a carrying case, decorate your drumsticks, or have something special to wear when drumming.

Consider keeping a drum for your personal use. It can be a good decision. When we think of community building, there's often a tendency to equate that with sharing everything, and to interpret a sense of ownership as selfishness. But a strong fabric is not made of threads all going in the same direction. A strong community is a blend of the personal and the communal. And a drum circle, even if drumming is all you do together, is a community. A drum, or any instrument for that matter, can be a very personal thing. Go with your own intuition where sharing is concerned. Do what feels right for you. As you grow, share your discoveries, your visions, and your expectations with the group. By drumming together, we have an opportunity to learn not only about rhythm, but also about leadership, sharing, listening to one another, and teamwork.

Circle drumming is a potentially powerful force in unifying a community, but it can also be a very personal experience—sometimes both at the same time. I find it's like putting a zoom lens on my inner eye, focusing attention on my personal experience while staying aware of the larger circle, and vice versa. Balance your drumming experience with time alone as well as in a group. Experiment with different roles: lead, follow, back beat, improvise. Let your drumming time be a free space to reinvent yourself.

Rattles and Other Percussion Instruments

Sticks, rattles, bells, chimes, castanets, marimbas, table tops, water jugs, rocks...Just about anything you can make a noise with becomes a musical instrument in the right hands. The twentieth century composer, John Cage, is famous for building instruments from all sorts of "junk," in order to achieve the kinds of sound he needed for a piece of music.[2] I once saw inmates at the Maui County Correctional Facility put on a skit using maracas made of empty soda cans and rice, and a children's drum circle where many of the drums were Rubbermaid containers. They both sounded great. In your adventures with percussion, don't neglect the many tools at your fingertips.

Like drumming, the use of rattles is an ancient vehicle for spirit work, attributed to purification,[3] calling for spirit guides and protection,[4] eliciting a shamanic state of consciousness,[5] and "clearing our rigidity, limitations, and old forms."[6] My own experience with rattles has shown me they are a perfect counterpart to drums as tools for spiritual work, like a scrub brush for the aura, and a wake up call for the psyche.

Of Drums and Drummers

A drum is a container for energy; what you put into it is available to you in return. Drums are also powerful transmitters. The energy you put into a drum—by playing it, by taking care of it, by bringing your highest and best to your drumming—radiates outward in the vibrations you send forth. So consider how you treat your drum, whether you are playing it or not. Where do you store it, what state of mind do you bring to it, how do you use it in your life?

Keep in mind that when you drum, your influence reaches far beyond your immediate circle. Children, neighbors, animals, plants, the very Earth, all absorb the energy you are generating when you drum. A short experiment will illustrate this. Play a simple heartbeat on your drum, Ka-dung, Ka-dung, Ka-dung, Ka-dung. Stay with it for a minute or two, long enough for your body to fall into the rhythm as if you were walking or rocking in a comfortable chair, Ka-dung, Ka-dung. Then, suddenly leap into some arrhythmic, helter-skelter pounding and just see how it feels. Now, stop the banging noise and go back to an even Ka-dung, Ka-dung, Ka-dung, Ka-dung. What was that like? If it was jarring for you, imagine how unsettling it might feel for someone who wasn't expecting you to disrupt the rhythm that way. We influence our surroundings by the sounds we produce.

Children are drawn to drumming like a magnet. Think of a baby in a high chair, pounding away on the tray-table. They love it. Put a drum under those little hands and watch what happens! By surrounding a drum with the sense of awe and wonderment accessible to most youngsters, you can teach kids to approach a drum with respect. Develop simple habits for them to integrate into their drumming rituals, like greeting the drum and handling it in a good way. With a bit of guidance, many kids will be able to drum with a group, and start learning the principles and techniques in this book.

In this multicultural world we inhabit, many different traditions and belief systems are all intersecting here and now. Sometimes it is challenging to sift through apparently conflicting values to find our own understanding of truth. In my experience, the more I turn my attention to living in a sacred manner by treating everything and everyone with respect and reverence, the better I feel. Part of walking that talk is living with the assumption that others are doing the best they can to find the way back to their sacredness, no matter how things might look at the moment. Sometimes I see beautiful drums treated in ways that feel so improper to me. Yet I have to remember where I am and understand that the journey toward right relationship with all things is a process, one I also struggle with daily. Each of us has to find our own way, to learn when to speak up, and when simply to accept that which we do not understand.

I think of my drums as personal friends or relatives. Some I see as an altar, especially a Mother Drum. I strive for personal equanimity, and insist on an absence of substance abuse in the circle. I create designs in cornmeal and tobacco, and make prayers before drumming, asking for the highest and best for All Our Relations. There have been times I've answered an invitation by taking the Mother Drum to a gathering and never brought her out of my car, because the energy of the circle didn't feel appropriate. Trust your intuition. Like physical muscles, it grows stronger with exercise.

As long as you maintain an environment of sacredness and respect, you are on the right track. It has been said that "a butterfly stirring the air today in Peking can transform storm systems next month in New York."[7] Imagine then, the forces influenced by the relative roar of even the smallest drum. Taking something seriously doesn't always mean acting serious, though. Sacred space doesn't have to be dull or subdued. We are here to enjoy life and one another. Drumming is by nature a celebration. Let it be.

CHAPTER 4

THE BASIC ELEMENTS
OF CEREMONY

SACRED SPACE

> *Ritual is one of the oldest ways to mobilize the power of community for healing. It makes the caring of community visible, tangible, real...Ritual helps us see and experience something which is already real, hidden in the obvious. In fact, all of life can become ritual. When it does, our experience of life changes radically and the ordinary becomes consecrated.*[1]

> Rachel Naomi Remen, M.D.
> *Kitchen Table Wisdom*, Riverhead Books

Where is sacred space? It is set apart from the pursuits and constraints of mundane, everyday life in a time outside of time. It can manifest in a crowded bus or a pristine grove, in a congregation or a moment of solitude. Though we cannot describe it in the concrete terms of time and place, sacred is one of those words we seem to share a subjective understanding of, based on personal experience. Of course it is possible to drum without creating a context of sacred space. Rhythm can be rewarding for its own sake. But there is an ancient and primal quality to rhythm that insinuates itself whether or not we recognize it on a conscious level. Anyone who drums for long enough will probably perceive some experience of spiritual dimensions, regardless of their original purpose.

Scholars have grappled for centuries with the daunting task of describing *the sacred*. Dictionary definitions reveal as much about the perspective of the ones defining the term "sacred," as of the word itself. But we are here to drum. So instead of offering yet another attempt to define it, here are some qualities of the experience of sacred space:

- A time and place set apart from everyday activities
- A sense of awe and reverence
- Recognition that there are energies present, beyond our power to fully comprehend, and that it is nevertheless possible for us to communicate—even act in partnership—with those energies

How do we make contact with that other dimension? One very effective way is through ceremony. Ceremony combines reflection, words, and actions as a means of communication with one another, our own unconscious, and with the Divine.

CREATING A CEREMONY

Just as we have been taught to assign the role of music making to identified *musicians*, we have also grown accustomed to leaving ceremony building to other kinds of experts. For centuries, organized religions have used the tools described here to provide a structure for approaching spiritual dimensions. Unfortunately, we tend to cherish most what we have worked for and earned ourselves. Consequently, we run the risk of losing the energy of a ritual by going through the motions without understanding what is happening. We all have our particular talents and, of course, there are times when it is most appropriate to call upon someone who is dedicated to making spiritual matters more accessible to the rest of us. On the other hand, each of us has our own, unique ways of moving through life: drawing from a mixture of heritage, personality, and experience.

Creating ceremonies of our own can be deeply personal and empowering, bringing sacred space into our daily activities. Life cycle events, the changing moons and seasons, important choices and challenges, even the beginning or ending of a job, are all experiences we can respond to more effectively with the support of ceremony. As we take on more responsibility for our role in creating sacred space—creating a space for sacredness—we become co-creators in the process of reclaiming the wholeness (holiness) so at risk in our modern lives.[2] By trusting our own innate spiritual wisdom, we strengthen the connection to our Essence[3] and open a doorway to the magic of synchronicity.[4]

So what *makes* a ceremony? The basic elements are very simple. The power is not in how spectacular or complex a ceremony is, but in the *focus* and *intention* the celebrants bring to the occasion. A ceremony can be grand, even global, or private and subtle; it may last a brief, seamless moment, or span hours—even days. Just saying a blessing is a little, tiny ceremony. Ute Grandmother Bertha Grove once described to me how she makes an offering in a restaurant by silently taking a morsel of food and setting it aside on her plate. The *intention* is there, as she takes the time to stop and sanctify a moment simply by expressing gratitude. "Of course, they don't eat the *food*, you know," she said. "They are fed by the gift." The Talmudic sage Rabbi Meir used to say we should utter a hundred blessings a day—imagine it!

The phases of a ceremony can be broken down into five elements. We consecrate the time and place, define the purpose of our action in our dedication, do what we have come to do (ritual action), acknowledge and recognize what we have done, and formally bring the activity to a close. When planning and enacting a ceremony, imagine that you are in the presence of a wise elder to determine what is appropriate.

Consecration ▶ Dedication ▶ Ritual Action ▶ Integration ▶ Closing

Picture a wedding. Witnesses arrive dressed in ceremonial attire. The celebrants appear in procession, often accompanied by evocative music (perhaps Mendelssohn or Wagner). The person officiating may begin with the words, "Dearly Beloved, we are gathered here together today..." There are prayers and vows, and rings exchanged. The couple kisses, turns, faces the congregation, and ceremonially departs in a transformed state.

It is important to be authentic in our ceremonies. Drumming often carries with it images (and stereotypes) of indigenous people, dressed in traditional costumes and singing songs that have been carried down for generations. It's easy to make the leap that if we are going to drum, we need to look and sound the same way. For each of us, the interplay between tradition and experimentation can be a delicate edge to tread.

Since my personal background in drumming is grounded in cultures not my own, I strive to find ways of honoring the traditions I have learned from, both by holding their teachings sacred, and by not attempting to copy their traditional practices. Instead, I try to understand the underlying teachings and interpret them in the context of my own heritage.

> *When in doubt*
> *as a rule*
> *take the teachings*
> *not the tools*

As we move through the steps of a ceremonial cycle, remember that the components of each step may appear in different order or merge into one action. The entire sequence may last a moment, or extend over a longer period of time. Like a good recipe, this is both a checklist and an invitation to experiment. The message is:

> *Be yourself.*

Consecration: Defining Sacred Space

The process of defining sacred space is analogous to climbing a flight of stairs, each step carrying one higher and higher, into a different plane of consciousness.

Purification: We begin with purification. Depending on your background, this may be accomplished with the smoke of sage or incense, steam, water, breathing, a prayer, or some other activity. Perhaps it means ritual bathing and dressing in special clothes. It can be as simple as remembering to stop and take a deep breath before continuing.

Orientation: Although sacred space is not defined by time or place, the paradox is that we begin a ceremony by making such a distinction.[5] Setting a Medicine Wheel, or invoking the

Archangels or Directions, are methods of defining sacred space wherever we may be. Entering a house of worship and acting in a certain way (such as bowing, kneeling, or putting on a hat) designates a time of sacredness. Even Moses responded to the Divine call by answering, "hineini," *here I am*. A location may be "sacred" because of historic events or practices (for example, Stonehenge), or because of a naturally occurring energy perceptible there (such as the Grand Canyon). It is also possible to consecrate a place/time by calling in the sense of awe through rituals as simple as wrapping in a prayer shawl, or joining hands in a circle to pray. By including our ancestral history in some way, we also orient ourselves time-wise in the cycle of life.

We tend to think spatially, even when we are talking about time: our language moves us back and forth through time as well as space ("down through the ages"). When we orient ourselves for a ceremony, we are using that same linguistic trick: making a spatial distinction between a secular and sacred location, though we may not move anything but our awareness. In defining the space, we include ourselves in the setting. Orienting terms like north, east, south, or west are all relative. Wherever we are, we take those directions with us. It is as if we each are the nucleus of an atom, an energetic center point around which all else spins. Each of us, in our own, unique way, is in the center,[6] and "that center serves as our point of interaction with the sacred."[7]

Attunement: An opening song or prayer can be much like installing software that sends a signal to our inner being, tuning the internal communications system like a radio dial to the frequency of sacred space. If this activity is done in a group, it has the added dimension of inter- as well as inner-personal attune-ment. In sacred drumming, this could be accomplished by a spe-cial drumming sequence or a song honoring the drum, the Ancestors, and the Creator. A group might sing together, recite a prayer, or chant "OM." A shamanic drumming circle may drum, rattle, sing, and dance to collect their energies. Dressing in cere-monial garments, or setting candles, flowers, or personal sacred objects on a simple altar, can also help to anchor our attention.

Devotion/Offering: "An attitude of gratitude" is a good way to celebrate. Again, depending on your tradition, this may take many different forms. Offerings are symbolic acknowl-edgment of the Creative Force, and remind us that the gifting cycle begins with a giveaway. I struggled with the idea of bow-ing to a drum or making offerings of tobacco or cornmeal until I realized that all of these actions need not be interpreted as "idolatry," but as expressions of humility, reminding me of my place in the order of things. In an activity as dynamic as drum-ming, it is all too tempting to fall into the trap of letting things degenerate into an ego trip or opportunity to show off. Drumming is very powerful in ways we Westerners are only beginning to comprehend. At the very least, drumming effects all the biorhythms it reaches. Before such potential, we do well to be humble.

Dedication

Defining the Purpose: Ceremonies need definition. Terms like wedding, baby naming, and funeral, each send a clear message to all who will attend: what to wear, what to bring, how to act. Purpose and intention are very similar. I think of *intention* as the energy focused around a purpose—the degree to which we are willing to show up for a task. A drum session dedicated to a specific purpose gives the participants an anchor for their *intention*, so the group can work together as a team with a shared purpose. The more clearly we can define our purpose, the more likely we are to achieve the desired outcome. The process of definition begins with introspection: looking within, if not for answers, then at least for productive questions.

Drumming for its own sake can certainly be a satisfying pursuit. It is also possible to dedicate our drumming to a particular task, such as healing, unification, or expressing gratitude. In her DiRRiD (Dance in Rhythm—Rhythm in Dance) training programs, Heidrun Hoffmann begins group sessions with a brief meditation, encouraging participants to find a purpose to which their drumming can be dedicated. Simply taking a few moments to go inside and name what is "up" has the dual benefit of focusing attention on the here and now, and merging that named purpose into the drumming, somewhere beneath the level of the conscious mind. By letting go of something, we give it the freedom to come back in a transformed state. If I'm looking for insight, it is helpful to be as clear as possible about my question, and then give it over to the drumming practice. This doesn't always work, but often I discover that something shifts and before long, I am able to see an old issue with new eyes.

Declaration: Once you discover the feeling or thought that is calling for attention, the next step is to name it. This sounds so simple and obvious, but it is a very important piece of the ceremonial process. Just the act of naming a feeling, whether it is emotional or conceptual, is a victory. As they learn to talk, children begin with the names of things, and then gradually string nouns together with descriptors that express actions and qualities. In the same way, adults pursue deeper understanding of the inner and outer worlds through a process of definition. Finding just the right word or phrase to describe a feeling can help unravel a puzzle. Sometimes it is difficult to differentiate ourselves from our feelings. Even our language reinforces that, as in "I am angry" or "I am frustrated." Naming a being, feeling, or inanimate object gives it an identity. Then it is possible to refine a relationship: it is my feeling, our family, her drum. Once named, an issue can be introduced to the group, "bring it into the circle," by saying the word aloud. You might say, "Today I dedicate my drumming to letting go of my feelings of inadequacy," or "I'm drumming for flexibility." In this way, we take an important step toward bringing our vision or feeling into focus. You might also bring into the circle the name of a person who needs support.

Sit quietly and take a few deep breaths, riding them like an elevator into a peaceful, meditative state. Think of yourself as an island, and of your feelings as passing weather. Ask yourself for a weather report—what you are feeling right now. Take a few moments to give that feeling a name, such as relaxed, frustrated, surprised, confused, tickled, and so on. Test out possible names until you find the one that feels right.

Ritual Action

Action: This is the centerpiece of the ceremony. In a sacred drum circle, the activity may simply be drumming. Shamanic groups may dedicate some or all of this time to trance work.

A meditation group may sit in silence. Structure this time to meet the needs of the occasion.

- Life-cycle passages may include a change of appearance or other public demonstration of the transition.
- Seasonal ceremonies may focus on symbols from nature, such as harvest images in autumn, light images in winter, rebirth images in spring, and abundance in summer.
- Healing ceremonies often include a physical or spiritual cleansing or symbolic letting go or release.

"What we imagine, we experience...Imagery is the way the mind and body talk to each other."[8] Imagery (symbolism) is fundamental to ceremony, because it bypasses the intellect and communicates directly with the unconscious through a kind of sign language. By creating a link between what we can easily do (for example, jumping from a chair to the floor) and what we want to do (taking a leap of faith), we can extend our beliefs about what is possible.[9]

Witnessing: We can perform rituals alone. On the other hand, taking action in the presence of witnesses can be empowering in several ways.

- Visions become more tangible when they are shared with others.
- Supportive witnesses strengthen commitment by adding their energy to the intention.
- We tend to be more focused when others are watching.
- As Angeles Arrien has put it, "When we are witnessed by three or more people, we cannot go back to how we were before. Both the witness and witnessed are changed by the experience."[10]

Integration

Affirmation: Oddly enough, an action is not complete until it is sealed in some way, like hitting "save" on a computer, or tying a knot at the end of a seam. Saying "amen" at the end of a prayer is an example of such an affirmation. In traditional Hawaii, they say *"amama, ua noa,"* "the prayer is finished." Wicca teaches us to slap the ground three times with open palms declaring, "it is done, it is done, it is done!" In a wedding we hear, "I now pronounce you..."

Tangible Symbolism: A ceremony may be a brief moment in time. How, then, do we keep the experience from melting away into a sea of memories to be forgotten? By carrying a visible reminder back into "ordinary reality"; something to anchor ourselves into a "new" frequency, or remind us of a commitment. An athlete's "lucky hat" could carry the energy of a particularly successful game through an entire season; a tiny pebble may take us back to a promise made at a sacred site. Some tangible symbols—like a wedding ring or badge of office—are not only personal reminders, they also make a public statement regarding commitment or status. Photographs can be reminders of a special event if they convey some key element of the experience, though an image is a different kind of anchor than a physical object. Words, phrases, poems, prayers, gestures, colors, movements, smells, and sounds can evoke the memory of an event and keep a feeling vivid in our experience.

Tangible symbolism can also mean that something is given away to another person or back to nature, as when the heroine of James Cameron's *Titanic* silently drops her necklace into the sea in a gesture of release and completion. Native American ceremonies often end with the exchange of precious objects, which strengthens the group's connectedness.

Closing

Arrival: Each ending is also a beginning. In a closing, we pause and consider this new point of arrival, for example, when the wedding couple turns to greet the congregation before leaving the consecrated space, perhaps hearing their names transformed for the first time. It is a moment of *here we are.*

Benediction: "Merry meet and merry part, and merry meet again, blessed be!" is a traditional closing benediction from the British Isles. If there was an invocation at the beginning of the ceremony (such as calling ancestors or directions), it is important to express appreciation and farewell at the closing of the ceremony. A group may have a particular song of blessing, which simultaneously strengthens the whole, while easing the process of separation. And, most importantly, benediction reaffirms that the wholeness (holiness) of the circle is not broken as we depart, but is carried with us and by us out into the world.

Diné (Navajo) Benedictory Chant

Now, talking God,
I walk with Your limbs,
Your legs carry forth my body,
Your mind thinks for me,
Your voice speaks through my lips:
Beauty is before me, and
Beauty behind me,
Above and below me

Hovers the beautiful.
I am surrounded by it,
I am immersed in it.
In my youth, I am aware of it, and in old age,
I shall walk, quietly, the beautiful trail.
In beauty, it is begun.
In beauty, it is ended.[11]

Bringing It Back Home

The process of integration may not happen immediately. Sometimes it takes years to understand an experience. The real work comes after a ceremony is completed (anyone who has ever been in a committed relationship is welcome to stop and chuckle)! Over the years, I have learned to talk less and less about my *non-ordinary reality* experiences, unless asked a direct question. These kinds of experiences are difficult to describe. Our language is not very well suited to descriptions of inner experiences except in poetry. Also, experiences which seemed profound and dramatic within the context of a ceremony can often seem trivial or incongruous in another context. Like the recorded drum session described in Chapter Two, the experience is what matters, not how it sounds later. And a mythic image—like a Zen *koan*—is something dynamic, to be understood rather than explained.

Ceremonial Drumming

What does all this have to do with drumming? That's really for you to decide. It's very possible to have a wonderful relationship with your drum without following any of these steps. On the other hand, if you want to use drumming as a spiritual tool,

then this may be useful information for developing your particular spiritual container. In "The Care and Feeding of Drums"
there are more specifics, but let me tell you a little about how I
approach the drum.

If possible, I light a candle and burn some sage or incense. Before a ceremony with the Mother Drum, I make a
wheel of blue and yellow cornmeal
on the surface of the drum to
honor its heritage. I offer a
prayer to dedicate the
drumming session. This
might take the form of
sending love energy to a sick
friend, or asking how to proceed
with a project. I begin by drumming around the whole circumference

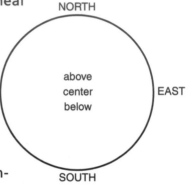

of the drum, honoring the seven directions: *west, north, east,
south, above, below, center*. This I do four times, rhythmi-
cally, listening to the drum as I silently repeat the names of
the directions. This serves two purposes: spiritually, it is the
first step of the ceremonial cycle (*consecration*), and practically this is a good time for a brief conversation to ascertain
if the drum is ready to sing and notice what qualities of
sound come from different places on the drum's surface.

I stop and listen for a rhythm to emerge. Sometimes what
arises is a song or phrase, that carries a rhythm with it.
Sometimes I drum the rhythm of a particular song or dance.
But at other times, I become very quiet and listen for whatever
rhythm is already playing inside me. Then I match it on the

drum, as if I am actually playing along with another drummer who is somewhere deep inside my Self.

I think of a drum as a great cauldron, and a drumstick as a ladle. With my drumming, I dip in and dip out *medicine* or energy. I'm not referring to drumming technique, but about my intention. This is the power of sacred drumming: whatever I am feeling is transformed into music. This does not mean that if I am angry I take it out on the drum. Always, always, approach the drum with respect. But through pouring myself into the drum, I am restored to balance.

When the drumming comes to a close—especially in a group—there is a tendency to finish with a crescendo, or cheer and clap once the drumming stops. This can be appropriate, especially if your purpose is release or completion. However, I usually prefer to come to a strong closing (remember "strong" doesn't always mean "loud"), and then drop into a silent, meditative space to absorb the fullness of the moment (*integration*). In a group, this can be the sweetest moment of all. Though it's not part of my ritual, I often kiss the drum, since it takes on the cherished quality of a dancing partner or beloved.

As I write these words, I think of my friend, Janice. I sat by her deathbed and drummed softly, humming familiar chants we had shared in drumming circles. The deep murmur of a simple heartbeat rhythm was barely audible, and brought with it a sense of serenity and timelessness. The room—and everyone present—became very peaceful. If you're not sure what else to do with your drum, hold it and listen. Be patient with yourself. There is sound in the silence.

CHAPTER 5

PUTTING IT ALL TOGETHER

It's time to take everything you've learned so far and braid it all into a single cord. Sacred drumming combines three themes, rhythm, ceremony, and drumming mechanics, into one activity.

DRUMMING ALONE

Sacred drumming is a conversation. Just as we could search a long time for the perfect definition of *sacred*, we could also linger over the question, "conversation *with whom*?" As your drumming experience grows, you may want to play with answering that question for yourself. But a conversation it is. Sacred drumming is as much about listening as it is about producing sound.

Develop your own ceremony for sacred drumming using elements that help invoke the kind of feeling you want to foster. Start your drumming with a rhythmic "walkabout" around the surface of the drum (described in "The Basic Elements of Ceremony"). In addition to the spiritual aspect of honoring the Directions, it centers your attention and gives you an opportunity to take stock of a drum's condition by listening to how it sounds. This practice is also my way of asking permission. If the drum doesn't sound right, I will attend to its needs before continuing (see "The Care and Feeding of Drums"). You may find that a certain time of day, or a certain place, seems to "bring out the best" in you and your drum. If I'm indoors, I like to turn off the ringer on the telephone to avoid being interrupted, and light a candle to invoke a sense of sacredness. Leave plenty of room for silence—before, during, and after your session.

Instead of telling you *what to do*, I'd like to discuss *how to be*—to address attitude rather than technique. For one thing, it isn't possible to give you an experience of drumming in words. Besides, I want to encourage you to discover drumming for yourself, not through a conceptual process of reading directions and trying to follow them, but by experimenting with the rhythms around you in the music you hear in your own inner and outer world. Find a rhythmic pattern you can follow, and allow it to take you on an adventure. You may find a simple *ka-dunk, ka-dunk, ka-dunk, ka-dunk* very challenging. If so, stay with it and see what happens. If you get lost, don't worry. Remember, rhythm bounces when you drop it, so just pick it up again and keep going, *ka-dunk, ka-dunk, ka-dunk, ka-dunk*.

Just like learning to drive a car, your mind has to teach your body certain steps. But once your body has learned, your mind can attend to other interesting aspects of the journey, like the passing scenery. Free drumming is a kind of meditation. Your objectives are the feeling it gives you, and the things you discover about yourself along the way. Like meditation, drumming can mean different things to different people. Give yourself permission to explore what works for you.

DRUMMING TOGETHER

Drumming in a group is both easier and more challenging than drumming alone. Later on we'll explore the logistics of organizing a drum circle (see "Starting a Drum Circle"). For now, let's assume that you and a friend or group of friends have assembled. You have drums, rattles, or other percussion instruments. You're eager to drum together. A combination of awkwardness and expectancy fills the air. How do you begin?

Remember what you learned about sacred space. Create a safe place to experiment and be a novice, perfectly imperfect. Light a candle, say a prayer, let go of everything but here and now. Let yourself drop into your own interior world. Take your time and allow a stillness to come over the circle. Someone begins a simple rhythmic pattern, and gradually others join in. Like a bird learning to fly, there are wobbly moments and times of gliding grace, followed by more confusion and coming back into the current. Just as you think you've got it, your thoughts tangle your concentration and you fall out of rhythm again. But somehow the group is undisturbed by your momentary loss of focus, and you are able to jump back in. Or, you all lose your concentration and the whole thing lands in a heap. So you laugh, regroup, and begin again.

This is free drumming. There may be someone who the group identifies as a leader. Better yet, this role may be shared in a more egalitarian way with leaders emerging from the group as needed. I often find that somewhere in the middle of a cycle there is a time of struggle, even chaos, as we work through the layers from planned to intuitive collaboration.

Personalities, proficiencies, and preconceived ideas all rise to the surface and need to be worked out. This is an aspect of group drumming I find particularly meaningful because this is the place beyond words. Here, we are unencumbered by many of the patterns we've developed for relating to one another. So, when cacophony happens, flow with it. Stay connected to your own center, and to the group intention. Chances are the wrinkles will shake out of the "fabric" and before long you will realize there is magic in the air. The circle has touched a place of greater connectedness. There you are!

Just as a bird learns to fly, it must also learn to land. Ending well is important, because it determines what happens to the energy you have generated while drumming. Sometimes the group dynamic will lead to its own resolution. Generally, closure is a time to check in with your drum buddies and, depending on what's happening in the room, rise to a crescendo, ease gently into silence, or come to a measured cutoff. The crescendo and fade-out are fairly easy to follow just by listening. But the cutoff takes a clear signal from the leader: facial expressions, gestures, or even vocal cues. A simple way to end together is to hold up your hand and literally count in rhythm with your fingers (and voice if necessary), "one-two-three-*four!*" The drummers end together on "four." That kind of crisp finish can give the ending an exhilarating snap, like a briskly shaken rug.

What you *don't* want to do is let the energy you created dissipate through loss of focus. If you feel the group is losing attention, try shifting the rhythm, speeding up slightly, or introducing some new element like a chant. You will find that it is possible to navigate the course of a drumming session in this way, and then bring the group around to a strong closing. And remember, sometimes the magic works, and sometimes it doesn't. Group free drumming is about unity, not domination. Be patient with yourself, and with the group.

When the drumming ceases, you have an opportunity to deepen the experience even more by becoming silent. You may find this is a good time for silent meditation. We have a tendency to leap from one experience to another when sometimes the best thing to do is *nothing.* Drumming can be so exhilarating that it seems natural to explode into cheers and revelry, and sometimes that's totally appropriate. But, just as applause may feel disruptive after an especially moving performance, outbursts of self-congratulation can pop an electric moment like a bubble, causing us to miss the precious gem of transcendence we've just invited. Don't rush past what you have just created.

MEDITATIONS

Here are some sample read-aloud meditations to help you set the intention before drumming alone or in a group, and to give you a few ideas for creating meditations of your own. You may want to incorporate these or other meditations into larger ceremonies. If you are working alone, study each meditation as if it were a map to follow later, or read the meditations aloud into a tape recorder for yourself. Before using one of these exercises, read through it and make any preparations you need in order to follow the steps.

Find a position that is comfortable for you: cross-legged or seated in a chair, standing with knees softly bent (not locked), or lying down if you can keep from falling asleep. Have the drums, drumsticks, rattles, and other implements ready and waiting so you can begin your drumming without disrupting the energy created by the meditation. You may want to keep a journal nearby.

Preparation for Beginning Drummers

Close your eyes and take a few long, deep breaths. Check in with your body to make sure it is comfortable and adjust your position if necessary. You might want to let your head, neck, and torso sway a little, as if you were a willow tree in a gentle breeze. Lay your hands peacefully in your lap, palms turned upwards, fingers relaxed and open. (Reader: pause here and allow time for the experience.)

Allow your breathing to find a deep, natural rhythm, and focus your attention on your nostrils, feeling the breath blowing softly in and out, in and out. Pause briefly between each out-breath and in-breath, as if you were pushing yourself in a swing: out-in-pause, out-in-pause, out-in-pause, out-in-pause. Take your time. Don't force yourself to take big breaths or hold air, just allow your breathing to find a full, relaxed rhythm: out-in-pause, out-in-pause, out-in-pause. (Pause)

Turn your attention to the base of your pelvis. Allow the steady pulsations of Earth-energy to flow into your body through your root chakra. Feel the energy rising up into you. Feel the life force glowing and radiating upward until it fills your torso like liquid light and spills over into your arms. Feel the energy trickle all the way down to your hands and out through your fingertips, collecting like balls of light in your hands, growing larger and larger until it becomes one big ball of light resting like a bubble into your hands resting in your lap. (Pause)

Feel your hands pulsating with light, pulsating in rhythm with the beating of your heart. Feel the rhythm of your body, the rhythm of Earth-energy pouring through you, bathing you inside and out with life force; steady, constant, alive. You *are* rhythm. Your body was born in rhythm, of rhythm, by rhythm, with rhythm. Breathing in, rhythm. Breathing out, rhythm. (Pause)

Listen to the rhythms you feel inside—in your body, your imagination, wherever the rhythms arise. Is there one that calls to you? Wrap your attention around whatever you are feeling; perhaps it is simply a feeling of pulsation. Let that sensation pour down into your hands and flow into your palms, into the ball of light you hold in your lap. (Pause)

Gradually move your hands from underneath the ball and slide them on top of it until they are floating like a cloud. Allow your hands to bounce easily with your rhythm. Play with it. You may even want to toss the ball lightly from one hand to the other in time with your rhythm. Let your head rock, your shoulders sway, your torso dance lightly with your rhythm. Perhaps you hear a word being repeated over and over in time with the rhythm; perhaps a song bubbles to the surface in your mind's ear. (Pause)

Gradually let your movements become smaller and smaller, until your hands are again resting gently in your lap.

Take your rhythm back inside you and let it echo in your memory until it becomes the faintest whisper. Take a deep breath.

And another…And another.

Bring your attention gradually back into the room. Let the rhythm continue to echo within you as you silently open your eyes and pick up your drum. Take your time to enjoy the silence in the room, the rhythm inside you, the drum in your arms.

Drum Dedication

Close your eyes and take a few long, deep breaths. Check in with your body to make sure it is comfortable, and adjust your position if necessary. Gently rotate your head and shoulders, breathing out any tension you feel there. Imagine your spine is a string of pearls suspended from your head. Sway the pearls lightly from side to side until you find that point of perfect balance where the pearls—your vertebrae—are effortlessly poised one on top of another.

Lay your hands peacefully in your lap, allowing the fingers of both hands to overlap, with the tips of your thumbs touching one another. Feel the current of energy running in the circle you have completed by touching your thumbs together. Take your time and allow the energy to build to a clear, comfortable hum. Allow your voice to pick up the vibration and center the soft rumble of sound in the sinus cavities behind your forehead. Imagine you are inside a great cavern—your sinus cavities—filling it with sound. (Reader: pause here and allow time for the experience.)

Allow the sound of your voice to melt back into silence, continuing to vibrate and circulate deep within you. Focus your attention on your breathing: a deep, natural rhythm. Focus your attention on your nostrils. Feel the breath blowing softly in and out, in and out, like Earth-breath in the great cavern of your sinuses. Enjoy the vastness of space, the gentle wind moving in and out, in and out. (Pause)

Your thoughts have melted away in the vastness of space. You have not come to think, you have come to listen. Here in the stillness, in the darkness of your cavern, you have come to meet the spirit of your drum. Explore your space, open all your inner senses. Take your time. (Long pause)

Let your awareness move back through any images, words, feelings, scents, or sounds you may have just experienced, and tuck them safely into your memory. (Pause) Now gradually move your attention to your hands. You may find that you are holding something—something that symbolizes your feelings in this moment. (Pause) Now, before you leave this place, take a few moments to express your gratitude in your own way—for your experience, for this moment. (Pause)

Take a long, slow breath. And another…

Gradually bring your attention back to the here and now. Return your awareness to your body and adjust your position quietly. Pick up your drum. Play softly, or sit in silence, as you wish. Ask your drum these three questions:

- What is your name?
- Why are you here—what is your dedication?
- What is your song?

Take your time. Play softly, walk, dance, or sit in silence. Be open to receiving messages in any form.

(After this meditation, you may want to share your experience in a circle, or write in your journal. Create a ceremony, alone or with your group, to introduce and welcome your drum to the circle. See "The Care and Feeding of Drums" for ideas on creating a drum dedication ceremony.)

Community Building

Close your eyes and take a few long, deep breaths. Gently rotate your head and shoulders, breathing out any tension you feel there. Check in with your body to make sure it is comfortable, and adjust your position if necessary. Focus your attention on your breathing. Exhale completely, emptying any stale air from the "bottom" of your lungs. Push out with a gentle puffing sound at the end of each exhalation. Notice how your next in-breath happens automatically when you exhale deeply and relax. Play with this process for a few breaths, letting exhalation become the beginning of your breathing cycle, allowing fresh air to flow deeply and spontaneously into your lungs, and exhaling again. (Reader: pause here and allow time for the experience.)

Let your breathing fall into a natural rhythm and turn your attention to the space directly in front of your eyes. Imagine a pathway stretching out invitingly before you. Feel the warm earth beneath your feet as you walk.

You come to a bridge and as you cross it, you pause to gaze into the brook beneath you. It is full of life.

On the other side of the bridge, the path continues a little further and then turns to the left, around a hillside. You come upon a gate, and enter a very special garden. There are sweet, ripe berries and brilliant fruit to pick. Each flavor seems to prepare your palate for the next.

After a while, you find a place to rest and fall into a kind of reverie. All around you are people in your community who you care about: friends, family, pets. Feel the strength of your community supporting you. See yourself simultaneously held by, and holding, the power of the circle. (Pause)

How do you envision your ideal community? Try to distill your vision to a single seed-word that captures the essence of your grandest fantasy. Imagine that the word becomes—literally—a seed in your left hand, and wrap your fingers securely around that seed-word, your vision of community.

How do you envision your ideal Self in community? Try to distill the image of your highest and best to a single seed-word that captures the essence of your Self. Imagine the word becomes—literally—a seed in your right hand, and wrap your fingers securely around that seed/word/vision of yourself in community.

Feel yourself simultaneously held by and holding your place in the community, enclosing two seed-word visions: of community, and of self.

Take a long, slow breath. And another... And another.

Gradually bring your attention back to the here and now. Return your awareness to your body and adjust your position quietly, feeling the energy of your seed-word resting in your two hands.

If you are doing this meditation with a group, take some time to share your experiences. (You may want to create a ceremony around the theme of planting your "seeds" in a community garden, either tangible or imaginary.)

Calling Vision

Close your eyes and take a few long, deep breaths. Check in with your body to make sure it is comfortable, and adjust your position if necessary. Let your head drop gently from side to side, front to back, and roll slowly around, first in one direction and then the other. Lift and lower your shoulders. Let your torso sway until you find the point of perfect balance. Take several deep, full breaths, each time dropping deeper and deeper into a state of relaxation. (Reader: pause here and allow time for the experience.)

Allow your breathing to resume a natural rhythm. Focus your attention on your nostrils and feel the flow of air moving in and out, in and out. Feel your eyes roll comfortably upward as if you were reading something on the inside of your forehead.

Imagine you are walking along a road. In the distance, you see it winding, up into the mountains. The day is beautiful. You have all the time you need. Before you know it, you realize you are looking back down at the valley below—the trail seems to have carried you effortlessly up, up, up into the mountains. A stream giggles playfully off in the distance, and fluffy clouds hang delicately in a canyon below. A great bird soars over the valley below, and you feel as though you could almost reach out and step onto its powerful shoulders.

But instead, the path carries you irresistibly onward, higher and higher until, quite by surprise, you find yourself perched at the very pinnacle of the mountain. Slowly, slowly, you turn around. In every direction there are panoramic views. You are so high, you can actually see the curvature of the Earth: a great dome carpeted with forests, meadows, fields, and villages. From here you see the patterns of life. (Pause)

Turn your attention inward to your deepest questions. Select one of them to carry with you to the drum today. Call to your guardian angels, ancestors, or helping spirits for guidance as you gather your question in your arms like a child and begin to make your way back down the mountain—back toward the here and now.

Take a long, slow breath. And another... And another.

Gradually bring your awareness back into your body and adjust your position quietly, feeling the energy of your question resting peacefully within you as you reach for your drum.

Conflict Transformation

> *This meditation and drumming practice is intended to be shared by conflicting parties, before engaging in any kind of dialog. Plan for plenty of time after the meditation to drum together without conversation. If there is a facilitator present, have that person guide the meditation and share in the drumming. Allow for the possibility of non-verbal resolution. If it is appropriate, begin with a prayer.*

Close your eyes and take a few long, deep breaths. Check in with your body to make sure it is comfortable and adjust as needed. You might want to stretch a little before settling into a comfortable position. Let your head, neck, and torso rock as if someone were gently rubbing your shoulders, or, as if you were a tree in a gentle breeze. Take several deep, full breaths. With each exhalation allow any tension in your body or mind to melt away, riding off on an audible "ahhh."

Let your breathing fall into a natural rhythm. Scan your body once again, easing your muscles, balancing your posture, and smoothing out any tightness left in your face or head. Feel your jaw relax, your cheeks soften, your eyebrows to become heavy on your forehead. (Reader: pause here and allow time for the experience.)

Imagine you are a tree. Roots beneath you reach like long fingers deep into the ground, creeping around rocks and between the roots of other trees. Feel how solid it is to be a tree—rooted. Feel your trunk, the concentric circles of your rings radiating out and out with the passing years. Feel your branches extending up and outward, home to birds and squirrels and butterflies. Let the sunlight and shadows play through your branches.

Allow your attention to climb up, up, up into the highest branches. From here you can see far and wide. You, and everything around you, fit together into the larger web of life. Take your time and enjoy having a "bird's-eye view." (Pause)

Feel yourself simultaneously high in the treetop and rooted deeply in the earth, strong and centered between the two extremes. From this expanded vantage point, turn your attention inward. Take a few moments to form the question or concern you will be taking to the drum. Keep it simple, concise, to the point. Don't drift off into excess details or projections.

Just find a word or phrase that captures the essence of your issue. (Pause)

Take a long, slow breath. And another… And another.

Gradually bring your attention back to the here and now. Return your awareness to your body and adjust your position quietly. When you are ready, open your eyes and reach for your drum.

Healing

Close your eyes and take a few long, deep breaths. Check in with your body to make sure it is comfortable and adjust your position if you need to. Focus your attention on your breathing, allowing it to flow in a deep, rhythmic way, in and out, in and out, in and out.

Allow your head, neck, and torso to sway a little, as if someone were gently rubbing your shoulders, or, as if you were a supple, young tree in a gentle wind. Allow your breathing to find a deep, natural rhythm, and focus your attention on your nostrils, feeling the breath blowing softly in and out, in and out.

Imagine you are feeling a desert wind blowing against your face: warm, dry, silent. Feel it in your nostrils, on your lips, on your cheeks. You become aware of a deep thirst. What are you thirsting for? What places in you need to be watered? What would it take to quench this thirst? (Reader: pause here and allow time for the experience.)

In the distance, you see a woman dressed in desert garb. She is beckoning you to come closer. As you approach, you realize she is standing by a well. She is holding out a cup for you, filled with water to quench your own personal thirst.

This is the essence of Shekinah, the feminine aspect of God; she is watering your dry places, restoring life, awakening your dormant creativity. You drink, and feel the water surging into every cell of your body: cleansing, restoring, and awakening your vitality. You drink and drink until your own personal thirst is quenched.

You offer the empty cup back to the woman, but she gestures to someone behind you. You turn and find a loved one who is also thirsty. You spontaneously offer the cup and discover it is full again.

As the images gradually fade, ask yourself, what have I been thirsting after? (Pause) What was in the water that so quenched my thirst? (Pause) Is there someone close to me who is thirsting after something I have to offer? (Pause)

Gradually feel yourself becoming aware of your physical body again. Turn your attention to your hands as you bring them slowly together, forming a cup in front of you. As you slowly return to this time and place, know that your cup holds everything that you need, with enough to share.

Take a deep breath, and as you exhale, feel your breath blowing you all the way back to here and now, and when you are ready, open your eyes and silently reach for your drum.

CHAPTER 6

STARTING A DRUM CIRCLE

We started drumming on the beach at full moon, and sent the word out to a small circle of friends. Each month my partner and I trudged across the sand, drums strapped to our backs, carrying armloads of firewood to a fire pit. Wrapped in coats and blankets, we of-fered tobacco, smudged with sage, and started to drum. A few friends would show up, and we would drum together until the drums went flat from the fog or rangers came by on their rounds to close the park. Gradually the circle grew. I was amazed when people drove for an hour or more just to hang out by a bonfire and drum. We didn't talk very much. We were there to drum.

The time has come for you to put out the word in your community, to "call a circle." But how do you begin? Whom will you invite? Where will you meet? How do you organize the group? In "Getting Started" we talked about three levels of attention:

- *First Attention:* the body
- *Second Attention:* internal or external task-at-hand

- *Third Attention:* holiness, holding the entire circle of life in awareness

Think of the Three Attentions as the *ingredients, recipe,* and *container*, respectively. The body (who/when/where) is your list of ingredients. The dedication (task-at-hand) is like the recipe, describing what you plan to do with the elements you are combining. The intention is the *container*, how you *hold the wholeness* of the circle.

ENVIRONMENT

First Attention: The Body

Selecting a group and finding a location go hand in hand. It may be that a few friends decide to form a drum circle and need to find the right place. Or, an established organization with its own facilities decides to add a drum circle to its existing programs. You may have a clearer picture of the people or the place, but once you decide to start a circle, the process becomes a dialog between your visions and your resources.

> *Although we lived in a tiny apartment that could neither contain a group nor provide an environment suitable for drumming and singing, the beach was only two blocks away. This was both a gift and a challenge: The location was easy to find and we certainly had plenty of room. Best of all, we could make all the noise we wanted. But we were vulnerable to the changing weather, limited in our activities by the setting, and accessible to whoever might come strolling down the beach. We*

never knew for sure who was going to show up, whether they had any instruments, or what—if anything—they knew about drumming or sacred space.

The location—Regardless of group size, there are a few basic things to keep in mind when selecting a location.

The group

Community is where we find "like kind," where we find the support, challenge, and accountability to hold to the path.[1]

Who is in your drum circle will probably depend on how a drum circle fits into the larger fabric of your life. These may be people you live with, pray with, or work with every day. If you already have some kind of spiritual community, you can experiment with integrating drumming into the activities you already share.

Like dance partners, "drum buddies" are not necessarily people you meet with in other contexts. I've had some very connected drumming experiences with people, without ever knowing their names. Look around you. Are there co-workers, classmates, fellow congregants, or people who keep crossing your path for no apparent reason—people you would like to know better? Perhaps you feel a spiritual affinity, and would like a vehicle for exploring a deeper understanding of one another. Or maybe you are simply looking for an enjoyable activity to share as a different way of relating with friends.

Is the environment drum friendly?—*Drum friendliness* has two aspects. The foggy beach described above was no more ideal for the drums than for the drummers. Unless you have a *Remo* drum, which is made of synthetic materials and practically in-destructible, fluctuations in temperature and moisture are going to have an effect on your drum. Remember that too much dampness or too much heat will impact your plans, so add this item to your checklist.

The other concern regarding drum friendliness has to do with the issue of sound. Some people love to listen to drum-ming, anytime, anywhere. On the other hand, I've had enough negative experiences with unhappy neighbors to grow very sensitive to this issue. We're here to create community, not problems. It's a pleasure to be in an environment such as the Black Tail Ranch, where the sound of drumming was an inte-gral part of the whole experience. I hope you have an oppor-tunity to participate in that kind of gathering. One of the things I learned, though, was just how far the sound of even a single drum can carry—especially at night.

By being sensitive to your environment, you can find ways of blending in, rather than standing out. I was able to drum at my friend's hospital bedside because I kept the volume of my drumming softer than the noise in the corridor. Take the time to tune in first, to the level of sound around you and the "mood" of the group you are about to introduce drumming into. Also, chatting with the neighbors can often avoid un-pleasant and untimely incidents later on. You may even dis-cover an affinity with someone where you thought none existed because you made the effort to reach out.

Is it accessible for everyone?—Ask yourself what is involved in getting to your location (the perfect setting is less ideal if it's at the end of a car-killer road), and whether you have adequate parking. Be sensitive to accessibility issues for people with specific physical concerns. Also, keep in mind that drumming has a way of calling people, so make sure that your setting meets your desire for privacy or inclusion. Do you want to limit the circle, or are you inviting everyone within earshot?

Does it meet the special needs of the group?—Think about what special needs might exist within your group. This could include things like seating, child care, environmental sensitivity, space for movement and dancing, restrooms, and a kitchen if there is going to be food.

What does it cost?—Sometimes using a location can lead to interesting issues around ownership, leadership, and control. Hosting a gathering and leading it are two different roles, and someone who is good at one may not be as qualified for the other. You might also consider pooling the group's resources to rent a space in order to provide the kind of atmosphere you want.

When?—Your *when* may be answered by *who* and *where*. You may plan to add drumming to an ongoing group activity, to celebrate an event such as a rite of passage, or to gather support for dealing with a trauma or upcoming challenge. If so, timing will influence how you integrate drumming into your activity or observance. In a one-time situation where participants may be unfamiliar with group drumming, designate a leader who gives clear signals and is able to guide group energy "on the fly." You might decide to invite someone specifically for that role.

Let's assume for now that you simply want to call a circle for the broad purpose of drumming together, and that you want it to happen regularly, say once a month. Obvious markers are new moon and full moon. Linking with the cycles of the moon can have remarkable results. For many of us, however, our cycles are not built around the moon cycle, but rather the business cycle of five days of work and two days of weekend. Our responsibilities and commitments change from weekdays to weekends. Consider the group's priorities when you make plans. Remember, as the group's level of commitment increases you can always make new choices.

If you are starting from scratch in the process of creating a drum circle, think of community building from the beginning. Call a one-time circle, create a sacred space, present your ideas, ask for feedback from the group, and see where it takes you. The *Resources* section at the back of this book includes reference books to help you in the process of nurturing community within your circle.

> *The beach was a fine gathering place in summer. But as the days grew shorter and the rainy season began, it was time to look for an indoor space. My partner and I moved into a cabin on the outskirts of town, even smaller than the apartment. We started getting together regularly with another couple from the beach circle. Before long, the four of us settled into an easy routine of supper, meditation, and drumming by candlelight. Eventually we added shamanic journeys. But by the time three of us had lain down and the fourth found a spot to sit and drum for the others, the tiny living room was full.*

During that same winter, we made a dream come true. Ever since my all-night drumming experience at Black Tail, I was determined to have a Mother Drum in my community. After much planning and a few failed attempts, we made the drum's rim and shipped it off to Brooke's [Medicine Eagle] brother, Rodney Scott, a builder of exquisite drums. Thanks to the hard work and donations from friends who supported the vision, Heart of Peace finally arrived: a beautiful double-sided frame drum made from two buffalo hides, large enough for as many as twelve people to play together.

One of the drummers from the beach circle lived in town and organized meetings in a large home. There, we had plenty of room to dance, sit comfortably, and stay as late as we liked, rain or shine. News of the group spread by word of mouth. Each month there were more and more new faces as I looked around the circle. Everyone brought their own instruments, if they had any, and some of us brought extra to share. The Mother Drum provided a focal point for the group drumming.

DEDICATION

Second Attention: What Are We Doing?

How you decide to structure your drum circle will be a direct result of your dedication.

Drumming for its own sake—Sometimes, all the group needs is a place to unwind, to express itself physically rather than in words, and connect with friends in a manner other than routine day-to-day interactions. Don't underestimate the value of drumming for its own sake. Celebration, pleasure, and an opportunity to sing, dance, and allow your spontaneous self to be expressed, are reasons enough to call a drumming circle. It's amazing how much pent-up energy we can release this way. All the "stuff" that seemed so important gets washed away in a river of rhythm.

Drumming as the focus of a spiritual support group—Drumming can provide a central activity for supporting spiritual growth and physical or emotional release in a safe environment. You might try to take a few minutes for silent introspection about a particular question, and then bring forth a thematic "seed" word to anchor your drumming for that session. A seed-word doesn't need to make sense to anyone but you. It helps you identify a feeling without the encumbrance of a lot of story around it. For example, I might say the word "shovel" to signify that I want to dig up an old buried something-or-other and turn it from garbage into compost. You may say a seed-word aloud or keep it to yourself.

Drumming to focus attention at opening/closing of other activities—Just as drumming can provide a container for the centerpiece of your circle work, it can also act as the "book ends," defining the start and finish of other activities. Conflict transformation is one example of using drumming as a non-verbal way to align our energies around a shared purpose. Groups meeting for shamanic journeys often use circle drumming and singing as a way to connect a circle in the beginning of a session, and then again to celebrate completion of the meeting's central goal.

Drumming as one aspect of a more comprehensive agenda— The drum circle may be central to a group's activity, or play a supportive role in a number of different ways:

- A drum circle can provide a rhythmical foundation for all the activities within a community. The steady heartbeat sounding almost subliminally throughout the camp at the Black Tail Ranch had a unifying effect on the entire group, day and night. Since the responsibility for sustaining the heartbeat was shared by all, the entire community was—in effect—participating in a drum circle.

- Drummers can provide a rhythmical foundation for a ceremony or dance. A circle of drummers may remain in that role for an entire event.

- In a ceremonial setting where each individual has a time of central focus, such as in a cleansing ritual, the responsibility of sustaining the drumbeat can rotate through the entire group, along with other support functions.

- The use of hand drums makes it possible for celebrants to drum and dance at the same time. Heidrun Hoffmann has developed a form known as Mandala Drumming, in which the circle of drummers sings and dances around a large Mother Drum in synchronized patterns, like a pulsating mandala.

There is no single right or wrong way. Keep referring back to your Dedication as you plan your own drum circle. Build your own answer to the question, "what are we doing?"

> *The circle in town grew and grew in strength as well as size, and finally leveled off at about thirty-five people, though not all of them came to every gathering. I originally provided much of the group's focus, by calling the circle and guiding the drumming. Gradually that responsibility spread, as a few of the others grew comfortable enough to guide meditations, offer prayers, and hold the focus during the drumming. I knew we'd come a long way when the circle continued to meet, even if I couldn't attend.*

INTENTION

Third Attention: Holding the Wholeness

You have defined the body: who/when/where. You have set the dedication by declaring your purpose. Now you are ready to begin. But how do you make your vision a reality? The very structure of a circle is egalitarian. But without organization and continuity, the energy of a circle becomes diffuse or lost.

Remember, we defined *intention* as "the energy focused around a purpose—the degree to which we are willing to show up for a task." Your *attention* is like a zoom lens in your mind, focusing on the different aspects of what you are doing. In the beginning of this chapter, we used the analogy of the Three Attentions as the *ingredients, recipe,* and *container.*

The environment (who/when/where) and dedication (what you plan to do with the elements you are combining) are relatively easy to define in concrete terms. How you *hold the wholeness* of the circle (your *intention* or *container*) is a skill that develops over time. You will need to learn how to lead—and how to follow.

The struggle for a perfect balance between structure and freedom is an ancient one, a constant search for the "harmony between order and chaos."[2] Hold too tightly and the circle becomes rigid and mechanical. Let go entirely and things fall apart. Could a body dance without both a skeleton and a soul? Holding onto the perfect balance point is like surfing, a constant interplay of your Three Attentions.

Leading a circle, whether or not there is drumming involved, requires you to find and set your boundaries by exploring your own comfort zone and weighing the group's priorities. My personal style is to have as little structure as possible, so the group energy can express itself through whatever rhythms appear from the "soup." I believe this works because of the time that is dedicated to building a strong container through prayer and meditation before and after each drumming sequence.

Another group leader may hold the circle's integrity by maintaining a closer adherence to specific rhythmic cycles, perhaps by relying on chanting or dance movements to provide the framework. It is also possible for a circle of experienced drummers to be so attuned to one another that the wholeness is maintained by an implicit communication web, connecting the participants in a deep, intuitive way. Sometimes you just *know* one another, without planning at all.

The key to maintaining the integrity of the group is the appropriate and dynamic interaction of the Three Attentions. If there is more strength in one area, you need less structure in another. I encourage you and your circle to strive for establishing a level of trust so that the role of leader can rotate throughout the group. In this way, everyone can experiment with the subtleties of navigating group energy and experience and learn from one another's styles. I think of leadership, not as control, but as expression. When leadership is a rotating duty, the rest of the group has an opportunity to practice supporting and empowering the leader's vision.

Leadership is a skill that needs to be learned. So is *followership*. Many of us equate leading with control and following with submission or powerlessness, but this is not necessarily so. Both roles can empower one another in a relationship based on partnership.[3] Sharing the position of leader is vitalizing both for individuals and the group. Nurture leadership within the whole group so it does not become burdensome or monotonous. Experiment and talk within the group about your discoveries, both as leader and follower. Reach beyond what you already know how to do. As long as you maintain an environment of sacredness and respect, there is no right or wrong way to proceed in your path of discovery.

> *Time passed. Although the larger circle was clearly filling an important need in the community for a loosely structured opportunity for*

novice drummers to leap in and experiment, I missed the depth and intimacy of a small, committed group. Sometimes people came but seemed more interested in socializing, and lingered around the kitchen to talk when others wanted to drum. I felt the side talk and socializing leaked energy from the group. I struggled over how much to adhere to my own expectations. As carrier of a large and powerful ceremonial drum, I felt both protective and responsible for the kind of energy transmitted through it by the circle.

Although there is no single right or wrong way to run a circle, there are some pitfalls I've learned to watch for over the years. When issues come up, keep referring back to your Three Attentions as you make choices regarding what you feel is appropriate.

Just as we are in the process of creating new ceremonies, we need to develop corresponding codes of conduct. Energy, by its very nature, is constantly in motion: magnetic, dynamic, and integrative.[4] In practical terms, this means we are either giving, absorbing, or balancing energy. Cross-talk and outside conversations can be very distracting and deplete the cohesiveness of the group. One of the biggest challenges I run into is the tendency many people have to draw attention away from a purpose through unnecessary conversation. It's amazing how many people can sustain silence for hours watching a movie, but find it nearly impossible to pay attention for even a short period of time during a ritual or drum circle. A key element in creating sacred space is *focus*. Come to an agreement in your group regarding when and how much to talk.

To eat or not to eat: That is a question. Very often when we gather together, food is involved in one way or another. This can be a good—even important—part of sharing time together. Refer again to your Three Attentions when deciding whether or not to make a meal or snack part of your event. Unless food is specifically part of a ceremony (or meeting someone's special needs), it's better to keep eating and drumming separate. There are practical as well as spiritual reasons for this. Food can become a great magnetic force in a group and take the focus away from the central purpose of a gathering. Maybe a meal is exactly what the group needs. Just be clear on why you have gotten together.

Sometimes there are conflicting agendas, for example, when I realized the town group was not meeting my needs anymore. For me it meant I needed to let go of this activity. I eventually dropped out since it was clear that the majority of participants fit drumming into their priorities differently than I did. As we experiment with energy and leadership, we are likely to discover unexpected bits of personality flotsam and jetsam. We may get into power struggles, issues of ownership, feelings of inadequacy, and other sorts of things. The thing to remember is that we are all here to learn, to grow, to express, and to support one another in that process. *Maintain an environment of sacredness and respect. Then you can feel free to proceed on your own path of discovery.*

The issue of ownership extends in particular to instruments. When I say "my drum," I mean it in the same way as "my spouse" or "my child"—not that *they* belong to *me*, but that *we belong to each other* in a relationship. Just as some human relationships are more intimate than others, I hold some of my drums and rattles in a more proprietary way than I do others. In general, assume that other people's instruments are private, and not to be played or even touched without asking first for permission. Have a designated location for instruments that are available to be used by anyone in the group, such as a basket or sharing blanket. Explain to guests that shared instruments are kept in a special place, and returned to it when no longer in use.

THE HEART OF THE CIRCLE

> *A circle is not just a meeting with the chairs re-arranged. A circle is a way of doing things differently than we have become accustomed to. The circle is a return to our original form of community as well as a leap forward to create a new form of community. By calling the circle, we rediscover an ancient process of consultation and communion that, for tens of thousands of years, held the human community together and shaped its course.*[5]

Ideally, we would have mentors passing down the wisdom of strong and supple traditions, raising a new generation of drum keepers who feel the support of their wise elders. There are places left in the world where this is so. But many of us are forced to find our own way, driven by a fierce longing to reweave what is missing in our lives. It is as if we stood among the scattered pieces of our traditions, each of us holding a fragment. I imagine us building our future from the recycled materials of our past. Ceremonies, rhythms, dances, and songs are re-emerging from the collective unconscious and are asking us, once again, to make room for sacred space in our lives.

What I offer you is not the path of any one tradition. My own teachers come from many different backgrounds. Though I have tried to hold to the spirit of their teachings, it is very important to take in what is offered and allow it to be like food, nourishing and becoming us, simultaneously transforming and being transformed. What nourishes us also becomes a part of who we are.

We are not here to imitate our past or attempt to copy someone else's. Experiment. Build new rituals and continue to breathe life into them in all your ceremonies. Listen to the whisperings of your ancestors and invite them into your circles. Translate their wisdom into words that have meaning for you, and allow your visions to bring new growth to the tree of your own lineage. Let your drumming and your circle provide you with an opportunity to expand into and express yourself as you are each day, in a constant process of becoming.

GLOSSARY

Anchor: a stable reference point or foundation

Ashiko: a large cylindrical hand drum similar to a conga, but tuned by a system of ropes

Aura: the energetic field surrounding living things, visible to some people

Bachi: a wooden drumstick without padding (Japanese)

Back beat: a steady pulsation providing a rhythmic foundation for improvisation

Bar: in musical notation, one complete rhythmic cycle

Baroque Period: 1600–1750 (Europe)

Bass clef: in musical notation, music written on the *staff* for the low voice (in piano music, it's often played with the left hand and usually signifies notes lower than middle "C")

Beginner's mind: approaching life with a fresh, open outlook (Zen Buddhist)

Bodhrán: a frame drum (Celtic)

Castanets: a pair of shell-shaped "clickers" usually made of hardwood that deliver a sharp sound when hit together (Spanish)

Ceremony: an action performed to create an atmosphere of sacredness or communicate a message of spiritual content

Chakra: an energy center or gateway (Sanskrit)

Clef: a symbol in musical notation written on a *staff* to indicate the pitch range of the notes written on that *staff*

Conga: a large cylinder-shaped hand drum with a tunable head (African)

Dedication: a declared purpose for which an activity is performed

Dhoumbek: a small hourglass-shaped hand drum (Middle Eastern)

DiRRiD: "Dance in Rhythm–Rhythm in Dance" a system for teaching rhythm; involving voice, movement, and drumming, developed by Heidrun Hoffmann

Djembe: a large goblet-shaped hand drum tuned with ropes (African)

Downbeat: the beginning beat of a rhythm cycle or *measure*

Drum carrier: a drummer

Entrain: to come into rhythmic synchronization

Ergonomics: body mechanics

Essence: the unique manifestation of life force in a person or thing

Flat: in drums "flat" means lacking in resonance; in music "flat" means below the desired pitch

Followership: the ability to follow and support leadership without losing the sense of Self

Free drumming: improvisational drumming

Harmony: different sounds made simultaneously in such a way that they complement one another (the opposite of dissonance)

Head: the skin or resonant surface of a drum

Intention: the amount of energy focused around a *purpose*

Koan: a riddle that is not meant to be solved because it is a pathway into the contemplation of the unknowable. "What is the sound of one hand clapping?" is a famous *koan*. (Buddhist)

Leitmotif: a musical theme used to identify a character or emotion—a sort of signal or reminder to the audience

Mallet: a padded drumstick

Mandala: Drumming a form developed by Heidrun Hoffmann in which participants simultaneously dance and drum around a large communal drum in synchronized "mandala" patterns

Marimba: a large xylophone with resonators (African)

Measure: in musical notation, one revolution of a complete rhythmic cycle, a *bar*

Medicine: the specific energetic qualities of a substance, person, place, or thing

Medicine Wheel: the map of Native American cosmology

Meter: the number of beats that go into a rhythmic cycle (*bar* or *measure*) and the value placed upon the notes for a specific piece of music

Métis: a name used by Native Americans of mixed ancestry to describe themselves, from the French word "half"

Mother Drum: a large double-sided frame drum, sometimes called "pow-wow" drum

Musical notation: a system developed in Europe to write down music and rhythm; *musical notation* or *signature* uses five lines and the spaces between those lines to signify particular notes. The notes are written with different characteristics to express relative time values and clustered into *measures* that contain a designated number of beats per measure.

Musical signature: musical notation

Offbeat: a weak beat in a rhythmic cycle, e.g., other than the downbeat

Ordinary reality: a shaman's way of referring to the way things appear when not in an altered state of consciousness

Percussion: sounds made by shaking or striking an instrument

Percussionist: a musician who performs with percussion instruments

Performance: to engage in an activity as a provider, as in performing for an audience

Purpose: the goal or reason for doing something

Remo: a well-known drum manufacturer specializing in percussion instruments made of synthetic materials

Rest: in music, an absence of sound

Rhythm cycle: one complete iteration of a rhythmic pattern, beginning with a *downbeat* and returning to, but not repeating it

Rim: the part of a drum's body that provides a surface over which a head or skin is stretched. A frame or hoop drum is made of a rim and a skin.

Ritual: a ceremony that is repeated for particular situations or purposes

Sacred: an activity or place characterized by a sense of awe and reverence

Samba: a rhythm from Africa (via Brazil)

Shaman: a person who is able to move between different states of consciousness for purposes of healing, information gathering, and communication

Shamanic journey: ritual(s) a shaman performs to enter and return from a shamanic state of consciousness and the experience the shaman has while in that state

Shamanic state of consciousness: a state of consciousness that makes it possible for the shaman to perceive and experience life through a different "lens" than is possible in *ordinary reality*

Shekinah: Shekinah is the feminine aspect of God (Hebrew, vb'fa) The "kh" sound is like the "ch" in Loch Lomond.

Skin: the head of a drum

Snare: a wire or cord stretched across the head of a drum to give a buzzing sound, or the sound that is made this way; nice if you want it, a *snare* can be very annoying if it is caused by a poorly stretched skin or a splintered rim

Staff: in musical notation, five lines and corresponding spaces used for writing notes and rhythmic instructions

Staff: the five lines upon which musical notes are written

Sufi: a mystic (Moslem)

Synchronicity: apparently separate events happening in a sequence as if they had been planned together as part of a larger pattern; intuitively being in the right place at the right time

Taiko: a dynamic form of drumming that originated in Japan (*taiko* = "drum" in Japanese)

Tar: a frame drum (Middle Eastern)

Tempo: the speed of a rhythm

The Goldberg Variations: a series of pieces composed for solo keyboard by J. S. Bach

Three Attentions: three "focal lengths" for the mind: 1) the body, 2) internal or external task-at-hand, and 3) the entire circle of life

Trance: an altered state of consciousness

Transpersonal: beyond the personal

Treble clef: in musical notation, music written on the *staff* for the high voice (in piano music, it's played with the right hand and usually signifies notes higher than middle "C")

Tscheh: a wooden drumstick with no padding (Korean)

Wicca: an ancient wisdom tradition of Europe and the British Isles

Notes

Introduction

1. Joseph Chilton Pearce, *Magical Child Matures* (New York: E.P. Dutton, Inc., 1985), 32.

Getting Started

1. W. Brugh Joy, *Joy's Way: A Map for the Transformational Journey, An Introduction to the Potentials for Healing with Body Energies* (Los Angeles: J.P. Tarcher, Inc., 1979), 13.

2. Li Shi Zhen, *Pulse Diagnosis*, translated by Hoc Ku Huynh, edited by G. M. Seifert (Brookline, MA: Paradigm Publications,1985), 61.

3. Thank you, Alice May Brock, wherever you are!

4. Leta Miller "The Art of Noise: John Cage, Lou Harrison, and the West Coast Percussion Ensemble." To be published in: *Essays in American Music 3*, ed. Michael Saffle (Garland, forthcoming, Spring 1999).

5. For a world tour through drums, see Mickey Hart and Fredric Lieberman, *Planet Drum: A Celebration of Percussion and Rhythm* (HarperSanFrancisco).

6. Brooke Medicine Eagle, *Buffalo Woman Comes Singing: The Spirit Song of a Rainbow Medicine Woman* (New York: Ballantine Books, 1991), 199.

Why Drum?

1. Heidrun Hoffmann, "DiRRiD" (Dance in Rhythm—Rhythm in Dance) Training, Pajaro Dunes, Watsonville, California March 12–15, 1998.

2. Leta Miller, "The Art of Noise."

3. Lou Harrison, "Tributes to Charon," *Selected Keyboard and Chamber Music 1937–1994*, ed., Leta E. Miller (Madison: A–R Editions, Inc., published for the American Musicological Society, Music of the United States of America, Volume 8, 1998), 15.

4. The line between composed music and directed spontaneous experience dissolves in the work of experimental composers, for example, Pauline Oliveros' *Sonic Meditations* (Urbana, Ill.: Smith Publications, 1974).

5. Mickey Hart with Jay Stevens and with Fredric Lieberman, PhD., *Drumming at the Edge of Magic: A Journey into the Spirit of Percussion* (San Francisco: HarperSanFrancisco, 1990), 163.

6. Layne Redmond, *When the Drummers Were Women: A Spiritual History of Rhythm* (New York: Three Rivers Press, 1997).

7. Hart et. al, *Planet Drum and Drumming at the Edge of Magic*.

8. For information on the Rhythm of Life Foundation, see their website at http://deadnet/band_members/mickey/rfl.htm

9. Up-to-date information on training and events by Heidrun Hoffmann is available on her website at http://www.dirrid.com or the old-fashioned way: DiRRiD, PO Box 7224, Santa Cruz, CA 95061-7224 (831) 454-1445.

10. Reinhard Flatischler, *The Forgotten Power of Rhythm* (Mendocino: LifeRhythm, 1992).

11. Rachel Naomi Remen, "Initiation: The Gift of New Eyes," Adapted from *Noetic Sciences Review*, Winter 1997, #44, pg. 14. Keynote address presented at the annual conference of the Institute of Noetic Sciences, "Questing Spirit," Palm Springs, California, July 11, 1997.

The Care and Feeding of Drums

1. Drum Dedication Ceremony is from Brooke Medicine Eagle.

2. John Cage, "A Composer's Confessions" (*Musicworks 52,* Spring 1992), 9.

3. Angeles Arrien, *The Four-Fold Way: Walking the Paths of the Warrior, Teacher, Healer, and Visionary* (HarperSanFrancisco, 1993), 26.

4. Sandra Ingerman, *Soul Retrieval: Mending the Fragmented Self* (HarperSanFrancisco, 1991), 68, 75.
5. Michael Harner, *The Way of the Shaman: A Guide to Power and Healing* (New York: Bantam Books, 1980), 64.
6. Brooke Medicine Eagle, *Buffalo Woman Comes Singing: The Spirit Song of a Rainbow Medicine Woman* (New York: Ballantine Books, 1991), 70.
7. James Gleick, *Chaos: Making a New Science* (New York: Penguin Books, 1987), 8.

The Basic Elements of Ceremony

1. Rachel Naomi Remen, *Kitchen Table Wisdom: Stories That Heal*, Foreword by Dean Ornish (Riverhead Books, 1997), 153, 284.
2. Christina Baldwin, *Calling the Circle: The First and Future Culture* (Bantam, 1998), 14.
3. Jean Houston, *A Mythic Life: Learning to Live Our Greater Story*, Foreword by Mary Catherine Bateson (HarperSanFrancisco, 1996), 127.
4. Jean Shinoda Bolen, *The Tao of Psychology: Synchronicity and the Self* (San Francisco: Harper & Row, 1979), 23.
5. Mircea Eliade, *The Sacred and the Profane: The Nature of Religion*, translated from the French by Willard R. Trask (San Diego: Harcourt Brace Jovanovich, Publishers, 1957), 24.
6. Ibid., 37.
7. Baldwin, *Calling the Circle*, 11.
8. Rachel Naomi Remen, *Healing and the Mind: Bill Moyers*, ed. Betty Sue Flowers, David Grubin (New York: Doubleday, 1993), 347.
9. Brooke Medicine Eagle, *Buffalo Woman Comes Singing: The Spirit Song of a Rainbow Medicine Woman* (New York: Ballantine Books, 1991), 200. For more information on integrating ritual action into daily life, see Brooke Medicine Eagle's audio cassette *Healing Through Ritual Actions*

(©1986), available through Brooke's office: #1 Second Avenue E.–C401, Polson, MT 59860; (406) 883-4686, or email <tapes@medicine-eagle.com>. See also Jeanne Achterberg, *Imagery in Healing: Shamanism and Modern Medicine* (Boston: Shambhala, 1985).

10. Angeles Arrien, "Cross-Cultural Shamanic Practice," Esalen Institute, February 21–26, 1993.

11. Floating Eagle Feather, *As One Is So One Sees*. (Denver: Humanity Press, 1983.)

Starting a Drum Circle

1. Christina Baldwin, *Calling the Circle: The First and Future Culture* (Bantam, 1998), 49.

2. John Briggs and F. David Peat, *Turbulent Mirror: An Illustrated Guide to Chaos Theory and the Science of Wholeness* (New York: Harper & Row, Publishers, 1989), 15.

3. Riane Eisler, *The Chalice and the Blade: Our History, Our Future* (New York: Harper & Row, 1988), xix.

4. Angeles Arrien, *The Four-Fold Way: Walking the Paths of the Warrior, Teacher, Healer and Visionary* (HarperSanFrancisco, 1993), 86.

5. Baldwin, *Calling the Circle*, 24.

BIBLIOGRAPHY

Achterberg, Jeanne. (1985). *Imagery in Healing: Shamanism and Modern Medicine*. Boston: Shambhala.

Arrien, Angeles. (1993). *The Four-Fold Way: Walking the Paths of the Warrior, Teacher, Healer, and Visionary*. HarperSanFrancisco.

Baldwin, Christina. (1998). *Calling the Circle: The First and Future Culture*. Bantam Books.

Bolen, Jean Shinoda. (1979). *The Tao of Psychology: Synchronicity and the Self*. San Francisco: Harper & Row.

Briggs, John and F. David Peat. (1989). *Turbulent Mirror: An Illustrated Guide to Chaos Theory and the Science of Wholeness*. New York: Harper & Row, Publishers.

Cage, John. "A Composer's Confessions," *Musicworks 52*, Spring 1992.

Floating Eagle Feather. (1983). *As One Is So One Sees*. Denver: Humanity Press.

Eliade, Mircea. (1957). *The Sacred and the Profane: The Nature of Religion*, translated from the French by Willard R. Trask. San Diego: Harcourt Brace Jovanovich, Publishers.

Eisler, Riane. (1987). *The Chalice and the Blade: Our History, Our Future*. San Francisco: Harper & Row.

Flatischler, Reinhard. (1992). *The Forgotten Power of Rhythm*. Mendocino: LifeRhythm.

Gleick, James. (1987). *Chaos: Making a New Science*. New York: Penguin Books.

Harner, Michael. (1980). *The Way of the Shaman: A Guide to Power and Healing*. Toronto: Bantam Books.

Harrison, Lou. (1998). "Tributes to Charon," *Selected Keyboard and Chamber Music 1937–1994*, ed., Leta E. Miller. Madison: A–R Editions, Inc., published for the American Musicological Society, Music of the United States of America, Volume 8.

Hart, Mickey with Jay Stevens and with Fredric Lieberman, PhD. (1990). *Drumming at the Edge of Magic: A Journey into the Spirit of Percussion*. HarperSanFrancisco.

Hart, Mickey and Fredric Lieberman with D.A. Sonneborn. (1991). *Planet Drum: A Celebration of Percussion and Rhythm*. HarperSanFrancisco.

Houston, Jean. (1996). *A Mythic Life: Learning to Live Our Greater Story*, Foreword by Mary Catherine Bateson. HarperSanFrancisco.

Ingerman, Sandra. (1991). *Soul Retrieval: Mending the Fragmented Self*. HarperSanFrancisco.

Medicine Eagle, Brooke. (1991). *Buffalo Woman Comes Singing: The Spirit Song of a Rainbow Medicine Woman*. New York: Ballantine Books.

Miller, Leta. (forthcoming, Spring 1999). "The Art of Noise: John Cage, Lou Harrison, and the West Coast Percussion Ensemble." To be published in: *Essays in American Music 3*, ed. Michael Saffle Garland.

Pearce, Joseph Chilton. (1985). *Magical Child Matures*. New York: E.P. Dutton, Inc.

Redmond, Layne. (1997). *When the Drummers Were Women: A Spiritual History of Rhythm*. New York: Three Rivers Press.

Remen, Rachel Naomi. (1993). *"Wholeness," Healing and the Mind*. Bill Moyers; ed. Betty Sue Flowers, David Grubin. New York: Doubleday.

Remen, Rachel Naomi. *Kitchen Table Wisdom*.

W. Brugh Joy. (1979). *Joy's Way: A Map for the Transformational Journey, An Introduction to the Potentials for Healing with Body Energies*. Los Angeles: J.P. Tarcher, Inc.

Zhen, Li Shi. (1985). *Pulse Diagnosis*, translated by Hoc Ku Huynh; ed. by G. M. Seifert. Brookline, MA: Paradigm Publications.

ReSOURCES

BOOKS

Drumming

John Amira & Steven Cornelius, *The Music of Santaria: Traditional Rhythms of the Batá Drums*. Tempe, Arizona: White Cliffs Media, Inc., 1991.

James Blades and Johnny Dean, *How to Play Drums*. New York: St. Martin's Press, 1985.

Michael Drake, *I Ching: The Tao of Drumming*. Goldendale, Washington: Talking Drums Publications, 1997. *The Shamanic Drum: A Guide to Sacred Drumming*. Bend, Oregon: Talking Drum Publications, 1991.

Sophie Drinker, *Music and Women: The Story of Women in Their Relations to Music*. Afterword by Ruth A. Solie. The Feminist Press at the City of New York University, 1948.

Alan Dworsky and Betsy Sansby, *Conga Drumming: A Beginner's Guide to Playing with Time*. Minneapolis: Dancing Hands Music, 1994.

Reinhard Flatischler, *TA KE TI NA: The Forgotten Power of Rhythm*. Mendocino: LifeRhythm, 1992.

Mickey Hart with Jay Stevens and with Fredric Lieberman, *Drumming at the Edge of Magic: A Journey into the Spirit of Percussion*. HarperSanFrancisco, 1990.

Mickey Hart and Fredric Lieberman, *Planet Drum: A Celebration of Percussion and Rhythm*. HarperSanFrancisco, 1991.

Töm Klöwer, *The Joy of Drumming: Drums and Percussion Instruments from Around the World*. Diever, Holland, Binkey Kok Publications, 1997.

David Locke, *Drum Gahu: The Rhythms of West African Drumming*. White Cliffs Media, Inc., 1987.

Bernard S. Mason, *How to Make Drums, Tomtoms and Rattles: Primitive Percussion Instruments for Modern Use*. New York: Dover Publications, 1974. A. S. Barnes & Co., 1938.

Layne Redmond, *When the Drummers Were Women: A Spiritual History of Rhythm*. Illustrated by Tommy Brunjes. New York: Three Rivers Press, 1997.

"Tabourot," *Rhythm Ghosts*. Austin, Texas: The Tactus Press.

Sule Greg Wilson, *The Drummer's Path: Moving the Spirit with Ritual and Traditional Drumming*. Foreword by Babatunde Olatunji. Inner Traditions Intl Ltd, 1992.

Shamanism

Jean Achterberg, *Imagery in Healing: Shamanism and Modern Medicine*. Boston: Shambhala New Science Library, 1985.

Tom Cowan, *A Pocket Guide to Shamanism*. Freedom, California: The Crossing Press.

Felicitas D. Goodman, *Where the Spirits Ride the Wind: Trance Journeys and Other Ecstatic Experiences*. With drawings by Gerhard Binder. Bloomington & Indianapolis: Indiana University Press, 1990.

Michael Harner, *The Way of the Shaman: A Guide to Power and Healing*. Toronto: Bantam Books, 1980.

Sandra Ingerman, *Soul Retrieval: Mending the Fragmented Self*. HarperSanFrancisco, 1991.

Circles & Leadership

Angeles Arrien, *The Four-Fold Way: Walking the Paths of the Warrior, Teacher, Healer and Visionary*. HarperSanFrancisco, 1993.

Christina Baldwin, *Calling the Circle: The First and Future Culture*. Bantam Books, 1998.

John Briggs & F. David Peat, *Turbulent Mirror: An Illustrated Guide to Chaos Theory and the Science of Wholeness*. New York: Harper & Row, Publishers, 1989.

Caitlin Libera, *Creating Circles of Power & Magic: A Woman's Guide to Sacred Community*. Freedom, CA: The Crossing Press, 1994.

Brooke Medicine Eagle, *Buffalo Woman Comes Singing: The Spirit Song of a Rainbow Medicine Woman*. New York: Ballantine Books, 1991.

Starhawk, *The Spiral Dance: A Rebirth of the Ancient Religion of the Great Goddess*. San Francisco: Harper & Row Publishers, 1979,1989.

Margaret J. Wheatley, *Leadership and the New Science: Learning about Organization from an Orderly Universe*. San Francisco: Berret-Koehler Publishers, Inc., 1992.

Rhythm and Life Attitude

John Miller Chernoff, *African Rhythm and African Sensibility: Aesthics and Social Action in African Musical Idioms*. University Press of Chicago, 1979

W. A. Mathieu, *The Musical Life: Reflections on What It Is and How to Live It*. Boston: Shambhala, 1994.

Stephen Nachmanovich, *Free Play: Improvisation in Life and Art*. New York: Jeremy P. Tarcher/Putnam, 1990.

AUDIO AND VIDEO

VIDEO CASSETTES

Jim Greiner, "Community Drumming for Health and Happiness," LP Music Group, 160 Belmont Ave, Garfield, NJ 07026.

Uncle Mafufo, "Basic Rhythms for Arabic Drum," Armando, PO Box 24, Capitola, CA 95010.

N. Scott Robinson, "Hand Drumming Exercises for Unifying Technique," Wright Hand Drum Company, 1/800/990-HAND.

Warner Brothers Studio, "The Ultimate Beginner Series Sampler," Warner Bros. Publications, Inc.

AVAILABLE FROM INTERWORLD MUSIC

Robin Andan Anders, "Voices of the Doumbek."

John Bergamo, "The Art and Joy of Hand Drumming," "Finding Your Way with Hand Drums."

Brad Dutz and Friends, "Have Fun Playing the Hand Drums" Steps 1 and 2. *Designed especially for all people, from ages 7 and up.*

Arthur Hull and Friends, "The Guide to Endrummingment."

Mel Mercier, with special guest Seamus Egan on Irish flute, "Bodhran and Bones."

Babatunde Olatunji, with Drums of Passion members, Sikiru and Sanga, "African Drumming."

Layne Redmond and the Mob of Angels, "A Sense of Time," Explorations of the Tambourine and Riq. *Previously distributed as "Ritual Drumming."*

Jerry Steinholtz, with special guests Julie Spencer and Ronnie Monaug, "The Essence of Congas."

Glen Velez, "Fantastic World of Frame Drums" (with Layne Redmond). "Handance Method," Steps 1 & 2.

WEBSITES

The Drum Lesson, http://quantumweb.com/robin/dles.html
Based on Robin Anders' "Voices of the Doumbek" (see Video section)

Drummer Girl, http://www.drummergirl.com

Jim Greiner, http://gate.cruzio.com/~jgreiner

Mickey Hart, Home Page:
http://grateful.dead.net/band_members/mickey/index.html
Testimony before the U.S. Senate Committee on Aging:
http://www.dead.net/band_members/mickey/senspeech.html

Healthy Sounds, http://www.healthysounds.com/
"Barry Bernstein is the Johnny Appleseed of Rhythm-based music therapy." —Mickey Hart

Heidrun Hoffmann/Dance in Rhythm—Rhythm in Dance,
http://www.dirrid.com

Holly Blue Hawkins, http://home.earthlink.net/~hollyblue

Arthur Hull/Village Drum Circle, http://www.drumcircle.com/

Kodo (Japan) Drummers,
http://www.sme.co.jp/Music/Info/KODO/index.html

Brooke Medicine Eagle, http://www.medicine-eagle.com/

Modern Drummer Magazine Online,
http://www.moderndrummer.com

Babatunde Olatunji, http://www.olatunjimusic.com

Rhythm for Life Foundation,
http://grateful.dead.net/band_members/mickey/rfl.html
Created to study and promote rhythm-based music therapy and to bring the magic of percussion to all.

San Jose Taiko, http://www.tiako.org

SHOPPING FOR DRUMMERS

All-One-Tribe Drums, http://www.allonetribedrum.com
1-800-442-DRUM (3786), P.O. Drawer N Taos, New Mexico
87571

Earthshaking Music, http://www.earthshakingmusic.com

Heartbeat Drums, Rodney Scott, RR 1 Box 650, Bradford, VT
05033, 802/222-5921

Learning Middle Eastern Percussion,
http://www.cs.cmu.edu:80/afs/cs.cmu.edu/user/mmbt/
www/percussion/learn-med.html. *A rich source of information,
with hyperlinks to drum-related websites, not exclusively
Middle Eastern styles.*

Interworld Music, http://www.interworldmusic.com
RD#3 Box 395A, Brattleboro, VT 05301, 800-698-6705, 802-
257-5519

Lark in the Morning,
http://www.mhs.mendocino.k12.ca.us/MenComNet/Business/Re
tail/Larknet/larkhp.html
World Musical Instruments, Books, Recordings, and Videos

Talking Drums Online Catalog, http://www.talkingdrums.com

Toko Imports, http://ithaca.gateways.com/market/toko/

Rockline: The East Coast Musician's Web Mall,
http://www.rockline.com/muslink/drumlink.htm
*Also has jumps to websites of many drummers, manufacturers,
and miscellaneous sites related to percussion.*

Rhythm Fusion, http://www.rhythmfusion.com
1541C Pacific Ave., Santa Cruz, CA 95060, 831/423-2048.
*Drummer's heaven! If you ever get the chance to visit this store
in person, you're in for a real treat. D'ror Sinai, the owner, is a
fantastic drummer who teaches drumming and performs
around the area. He also designs and produces percussion instruments. The website is a great place to find just about any
kind of ethnic percussion instruments you could imagine.*

Related Books by The Crossing Press

LifeChanges with the Energy of the Chakras
By Ambika Wauters

When we face up to the reality of change, we learn to accept its challenges with grace and renewed grit. We can alter our old movies-our old patterns-and gain insights into our nature. We then can be released from the past and find new, healthy options for our lives.

$14.95 • Paper • ISBN 1-58091-020-3

Peace Within the Stillness: *Relaxation & Meditation for True Happiness*
By Eddie and Debbie Shapiro

Meditation teachers Eddie and Debbie Shapiro teach a simple, ancient practice which will enable you to release even deeper levels of inner stress and tension. Once you truly relax, you will enter the quiet mind and experience the profound, joyful, and healing energy of meditation.

$14.95 • Paper • ISBN 0-89594-926-1

Pocket Guide to Meditation
By Alan Pritz

This book focuses on meditation as part of spiritual practice, as a universal tool to forge a deeper connection with spirit. In Alan Pritz's words, Meditation simply delivers one of the most purely profound experiences of life, joy.

$6.95 • Paper • ISBN 0-89594-886-9

Casting the Circle: *A Women's Book of Ritual*
By Diane Stein

A comprehensive guide including 23 full ritual outlines for the waxing, full and waning moons, the eight Sabbats, and rites of passage.

$14.95 • Paper • ISBN 0-89594-411-1

Clear Mind, Open Heart: *Healing Yourself, Your Relationships and the Planet*
By Eddie and Debbie Shapiro

The Shapiros offer an uplifting, inspiring, and deeply sensitive approach to healing through spiritual awareness. Includes practical exercises and techniques to help us all in making our own journey.

$16.95 • Paper • ISBN 0-89594-917-2

RELATED BOOKS BY THE CROSSING PRESS

Crystal Enchantments: *A Complete Guide to Stones and Their Magical Properties*

By D. J. Conway

D. J. Conway's book will help guide you in your choice of stones from Adularia to Zircon, by listing their physical properties and magical uses. It will also appeal to folks who are not into magic, but simply love stones and want to know more about them.

$16.95 • Paper • ISBN 1-58091-010-6

Essential Reiki: *A Complete Guide to an Ancient Healing Art*

By Diane Stein

This bestseller includes the history of Reiki, hand positions, giving treatments, and the initiations. While no book can replace directly received attunements, Essential Reiki provides everything else that the practitioner and teacher of this system needs, including all three degrees of Reiki, most of it in print for the first time.

$18.95 • Paper • ISBN 0-89594-736-6

The Goddess Celebrates: *An Anthology of Women's Rituals*

By Diane Stein

...this collection will stimulate discussion among readers interested in women's spirituality.
　　　　　　　　　　　　　　　　　　　　　　　　　　　　—Booklist

$14.95 • Paper • ISBN 0-89594-460-X

The Healing Energy of Your Hands

By Michael Bradford

Bradford offers techniques so simple that anyone can work with healing energy quickly and easily.

$12.95 • Paper • ISBN 0-89594-781-1

The Healing Voice: *Traditional & Contemporary Toning, Chanting & Singing*

By Joy Gardner-Gordon

An excellent resource for individuals seeking to understand and apply the potent healing powers of sound and voice that we all possess. 　　—Richard Gerber, M.D.

$12.95 • Paper • ISBN 0-89594-571-1

RELATED BOOKS BY THE CROSSING PRESS

Pocket Guide to Shamanism

By Tom Cowan

Are you intrigued by the mysteries of nature and the realm of the spirit? Have you experienced a magical or mystical occurrence? Perhaps shamanism is calling you. Bringing shamanism into your life can allow you to restore sacred ritual, gain insight, and live with sensitivity and respect for the planet.

$6.95 • Paper • ISBN 0-89594-845-1

The Sevenfold Journey: *Reclaiming Mind, Body & Spirit Through the Chakras*

By Anodea Judith & Selene Vega

Combining yoga, movement, psychotherapy, and ritual, the authors weave ancient and modern wisdom into a powerful tapestry of techniques for facilitating personal growth and healing.

$18.95 • Paper • ISBN 0-89594-574-6

Shamanism as a Spiritual Practice for Daily Life

By Tom Cowan

This inspirational book blends elements of shamanism with inherited traditions and contemporary religious commitments. An inspiring spiritual call. —Booklist

$16.95 • Paper • ISBN 0-89594-838-9

Spinning Spells, Weaving Wonders: *Modern Magic for Everyday Life*

By Patricia Telesco

This essential book of over 300 spells tells how to work with simple, easy-to-find components and focus creative energy to meet daily challenges with awareness, confidence, and humor.

$11.95 • Paper • ISBN 0-89594-803-6

Voices from the Edge: *Conversations with Jerry Garcia, Ram Dass, Annie Sprinkle, Matthew Fox, Jaron Lanier and others*

Interviews by David Jay Brown and Rebecca McClen Novick

Anyone aspiring to understand the new millennium will have to read this book. Every page explodes like an intellectual firecracker. —Robert Anton Wilson

$14.95 • Paper • ISBN 0-89594-732-3

RELATED BOOKS BY THE CROSSING PRESS

The Wiccan Path: *A Guide for the Solitary Practitioner*
By Rae Beth

This is a guide to the ancient path of the village wisewoman. Writing in the form of letters to two apprentices, Rae Beth provides rituals for the key festivals of the wiccan calendar. She also describes the therapeutic powers of trancework and herbalism, and outlines the Pagan approach to finding a partner.

$12.95 • Paper • ISBN 0-89594-744-7

Wind and Water: *Your Personal Feng Shui Journey*
By Carol J. Hyder

This book presents Feng Shui as simple suggestions that can be done on a daily basis-each page will provide information and a corresponding activity. Instead of reading about Feng Shui, this book will provide an immediate experience of Feng Shui.

$19.95 • Paper • ISBN 1-58091-050-5

Wisdom of the Elements: *The Sacred Wheel of Earth, Air, Fire and Water*
By Margie McArthur

Drawing on her knowledge of neo-pagan tradition, as well as Traditional Chinese Medicine, energy work with the chakras, and Native American wisdom, McArthur gives us keys to the intricate correspondences between the Elements, the planet and our psychic landscape.

$16.95 • Paper • ISBN 0-89594-936-9

A Wisewoman's Guide to Spells, Rituals and Goddess Lore
By Elizabeth Brooke

A remarkable compendium of magical lore, psychic skills and women's mysteries.

$12.95 • Paper • ISBN 0-89594-779-X

Women's Medicine Ways: *Cross-Cultural Rites of Passage*
By Marcia Starck

An excellent primer meant to help us learn to make these ritual actions.
—Brooke Medicine Eagle

$12.95 • Paper • ISBN 0-89594-596-7

To receive a current catalog from The Crossing Press
please call toll-free, 800–777–1048.
www.crossingpress.com